The Way in Africa

GEORGE WAYLAND CARPENTER

The Way

in

AFRICA

FRIENDSHIP PRESS NEW YORK

LIBRARY OF CONGRESS CATALOG CARD NUMBER: 59–6037

COPYRIGHT © 1959 BY FRIENDSHIP PRESS, INC.
PRINTED IN THE UNITED STATES OF AMERICA

Contents

Contents

. . . FOUR

Christianity, Race, and Nationalism—
the Patterns of Power   75

Contents

CHAPTER ONE

The Invasion of Africa

OUTSIDE THE TERMINAL BUILDING OF THE NAIROBI AIRPORT in Kenya, East Africa, there is a signpost with arms pointing in every direction and bearing such names as London, Aden, Cairo, Dar es Salaam, and Johannesburg. Scores of scheduled flights come and go every day, and passengers from all over the world rub shoulders there. Yet only a few years ago there was no airport at Nairobi, and a scant two generations ago the city itself did not exist.

There are people still living who can recall when Johannesburg, South Africa, was only a cluster of tents on Ferreira's farm where gold had been found. Today it is a city of a million people, and mountains of yellow sand—the waste that remains after the gold has been extracted from the ore—extend for eighty miles east and west along the Witwatersrand.[1]

[1] Frequently called "The Rand," it is a series of gold-bearing reefs.

1

THE EMPTY MAP

Only a century and a half ago almost the whole of inland Africa was unknown, unexplored territory. The vaguest rumors as to lakes, rivers, mountains, and peoples in the interior were taken as fact and solemnly drawn in upon maps that would otherwise have been largely blank.

In the year 1802 a geographer named Arrowsmith presented to the African Association, in London, a map of Africa from which he had removed all details that could not be verified. Morocco and Algeria were still quite well shown, the reports of Mungo Park and a few other explorers enabled him to plot some regions with substantial accuracy; but for the rest, except in the extreme south and certain areas around Portuguese possessions, east and west, the interior was an unmitigated blank. "Gentlemen," said Arrowsmith, in effect, "this is what we now know of Africa; get to work and fill up the map." [1]

If we ask why the map of Africa remained so largely blank for so long it is not hard to find the answers. The map itself supplies some of them. The bulging northern third of the continent—apart from the narrow coastal zone bordering the Mediterranean—is arid desert and almost uninhabitable. The Sahara Desert is as large as the whole United States and until the advent of airplanes it formed a most effective barrier. The Europeans to the north and the Africans to the south were completely sealed off from each other, although Muslim Arabs, accus-

[1] Adapted from Smith, Edwin W. *Events in African History.* New York: Committee on Africa, the War, and Peace Aims, 1942, pp. 13-14. Used by permission.

tomed to desert life, penetrated into the fertile Sudan in about the eleventh century. Their influence has been considerable in that region.

Access by sea was hardly less difficult. Neither deep bays nor navigable rivers open pathways to the interior. Although daring Portuguese navigators, seeking a route to the wealth of Asia, explored the whole west coast during the fifteenth century and rounded the Cape of Good Hope shortly before Columbus discovered America, they did not get far inland. Permanent European settlements were made only at Cape Town (1652) and a few other . points on the coast.

Climate was another barrier, for Africa lies squarely astride the equator. The sun can be merciless, and seasons of torrential rain are apt to alternate with long periods of parching drought. With the inhospitable climate went deadly diseases such as malaria, yaws, and sleeping sickness. Many of these were unknown in Europe and the traveler had no defense against them until the advent of modern scientific medicine.

Finally there was the barrier of human fear and enmity for which the Europeans, together with Arabs of southwest Asia and North Africa, were largely to blame. For more than three hundred years Europeans' real interest in Negro Africa centered in the slave trade.

THE SLAVE TRADE

We shall never know what the story of Africa would have been if the slave trade had not radically and permanently (up to our own day) distorted the relations between the peoples of European and of African origin. In respect to the exploration of Africa it meant that the European was to the African not a friend but a predatory enemy. Hence all roads to the interior were closed. "Stay by your ships and your stockades on the coast," said the Africans. "We will come and trade with you there. But you must not come to us."

Some of the coastal tribes, however, derived great profit from their position by serving as middlemen between European traders and the tribes of the hinterland. A notable of a coastal people would buy a caravan of slaves at an inland market center in exchange for barter goods from the coast. Then he would sell the slaves at the coast for more barter goods, making a profit both ways. Apart from slaves the most valuable African product was ivory, so profits could be increased even more by making the able-bodied slaves carry tusks of ivory and selling both carriers and burdens at the coast.

At this distance it is hard to imagine the effects of this evil traffic in human lives. Tribe was set against tribe far into the interior. Probably many more people were killed in the intertribal wars and raids than were shipped overseas—and at the lowest estimate the latter numbered several million souls. Travel became unsafe and the peaceful fabric of society was disrupted. Suspicion and enmity between tribes continued long after the overseas slave trade was suppressed. In my own early years as a missionary I remember talking with a twenty-year-old student who was returning to his village for a holiday. His journey would take him three days on foot. "Aren't you afraid to go so far?" I asked. "No," he replied, "now we have government and peace. We do not fear our neighbors. But my grandfather could never have gone so far from home. He would have been captured and sold as a slave. He would never have seen his village again."

In the sixteenth century the paramount chief of the Bakongo tribe was the acknowledged head of a domain extending some two hundred miles along the Angola-Congo coast and as far inland. For a considerable period the chief's power enabled him to guarantee safe conduct to trading caravans passing through his territories. To avoid the royal tolls that were charged, European traders on the coast began importing firearms for their own trading parties. Eventually the king's peace was broken and anarchy ensued. A modern sociologist would label this "social breakdown following cultural invasion." But whatever the label, the fact of change is not something new in the present but goes far back into the past.

FORCES LEADING TO CHANGE IN AFRICA

All this is background showing why the map of Africa was still so largely blank even at the beginning of the nineteenth century. Yet already three great forces for change were emerging that were to result in the filling of the map. These were political, economic, and religious.

Political Force

The ferment of liberty that found expression in the American Revolution and even more powerfully in the French Revolution produced political change of far

5

reaching consequences. The common people, long regarded throughout Europe as little more than serfs, discovered that when they acted together they were strong enough to overcome privileged minorities.

The democratic idea encouraged public discussion and free inquiry. It stimulated thought, sharpened resolution, and promoted the formation of societies, associations, and movements for purposes in the public interest. And, although its spirit is only now beginning to be fully realized in Africa, the slogan "Liberty, equality, fraternity" had overtones of obligation toward oppressed peoples everywhere that has been a continuing force ever since the French Revolution.

It was important for the coming age that a new gospel of liberty and equality had been proclaimed as the slogan of a triumphant republic. The American declaration of rights gave the cue to every friend of liberty in the old world. What the Americans had made of themselves by revolution the Europeans might become by a similar exercise of daring. The spirit of liberty took many forms . . . but once aroused it embarked upon a contest which is still unconcluded. Surviving the crimes of the French Revolution and the terror of Napoleon, it succeeded by the end of the nineteenth century in founding parliamentary institutions in every important European country with the exception of Russia.[1]

Economic Force

The economic force leading to change in Africa was the industrial revolution. Beginning in Great Britain with the invention of machinery for spinning and weaving,

[1] Fisher, H. A. L. *A History of Europe.* Boston: Houghton Mifflin Co., 1939, p. 791. Used by permission.

and with the development of the steam engine, mass production quickly spread into other industries and took root in Western Europe and North America. Steamships and railways revolutionized transportation, while the ever-increasing output of the factories demanded wider markets and larger supplies of raw materials.

One of the effects of the industrial revolution was to make travel easier and quicker, and thus to stimulate exploration and the migration of large numbers of people. Another effect was to put tools in peoples' hands and money in their purses, making it possible for groups of quite ordinary people to project and carry out undertakings that formerly could only exist by the patronage of the great. The modern missionary movement began as a series of such spontaneous popular undertakings.

Religious Force

The third great force leading to change was the evangelical awakening that began in the eighteenth century. In all the Protestant countries of Europe and America thousands of people experienced spiritual rebirth. New communions came into being and existing churches were to a large extent revitalized. The urge to spread the good news of the gospel, and Christian concern for those without its light, prompted the sending of missionaries and the formation of societies to support them. The liberating democratic spirit and the energizing forces flowing from the industrial revolution furthered and sustained this religious outreach. At the same time people of sensitive spirit were aroused to a new awareness of the evils of slavery. Their efforts gave rise to movements for the freeing of slaves and the suppression of the slave trade throughout the world.

THE INVASION OF AFRICA

These three great social forces converged on Africa in what can only be described as an invasion. The invasion is, in fact, still going on with ever multiplying effect. Whole libraries have been written about different phases of it. This book cannot attempt to tell the whole story. It will not deal with North Africa at all, for that is a different world linked to the middle East by the dominant Muslim faith. But with reference to Africa south of the Sahara, it will try to do two things:

1. Look in some detail at the present day outcomes of this invasion of Africa by the Western world.

2. Consider the meaning of Africa for us as Christians today—heirs both of Western culture and of the missionary outreach of the past, and responsible in some degree for the shape of tomorrow.

Colonization

Between 1800 and 1850 the slave trade across the Atlantic from the west coast of Africa virtually came to an end. During about the same period a few colonies of Negroes freed from slavery were established in Africa, notably at Freetown and Monrovia. Out of these were to grow the colony of Sierra Leone and the republic of Liberia. Explorers pushed farther and farther inland; not a few perished in the effort to trace the courses of the great rivers of Africa, which, as they vainly hoped, might serve as arteries of trade.

Equatorial Africa became known as "the white man's grave" because so few Europeans could endure its climate and resist its diseases. But missionaries came and kept coming. Though many died others came to fill their places, bringing schools, medical services, a variety of practical crafts, and plants that would eventually become the basis of livelihood of vast numbers of Africans.

The milder climate of South Africa had encouraged Europeans to settle there very early, the first group arriving in 1652. These first immigrants included many nationalities, but Dutch Calvinists predominated. From 1806 onwards, after control of the colony passed to the British government, conflict developed between the Boers (Dutch-speaking farmers descended from the early settlers) and the English who had come later. The Boers, now called Afrikaners, became increasingly infuriated at British rule and eventually large numbers of them migrated (1835-37) northward and eastward to find new homes. This movement brought them into conflict with the Zulu and Matabele tribes, peoples of remarkable military prowess, who were migrating southward into the same territories. Thus were sown the seeds of enmity and racial antagonism that persist to this day. The folk-tradition of the Afrikaners especially dramatizes their role in history as beleaguered defenders of freedom, who withstood the assaults of the British on the one hand and the African "savages" on the other. Only against this historical background can present Afrikaner psychology be understood.

Little by little the coastal settlements under various European flags—British, Portuguese, Spanish, French, and later German—became the basis for extensive territorial claims in the interior. Boundaries were drawn on maps, although there was often little attempt to control the territories claimed. Rarely did these boundaries coincide with the limits of tribal lands. Hence today there are many instances of peoples historically one, speaking the same mother tongue, but divided by political frontiers into artificial segments. Ruled by different governments, they learn different European languages, evolve under different policies, and live within different economic orbits. Sometimes this divisiveness has extended even to the sphere of religion, as colonial governments have, for political reasons, frequently shown partiality to a particular faith or confession. The political map of Africa, like so much else, was imposed from the outside with little thought and less concern for the people living there.

David Livingstone

Across middle nineteenth century Africa strides one heroic figure that dwarfs all others—David Livingstone. He typifies and embodies the dominant forces of the age in their impact on Africa. Born of poor Scottish parents, he was sent while still a child to work in the cotton mills. Determined to get an education, he studied while he worked, propping his Latin book on the spinning frame. He dreamed of offering himself for missionary service in

China, and studied medicine in order to minister more effectively to human needs. But when he was ready there were no openings for service in China, so he accepted a call to South Africa. There he met and married Mary Moffat, daughter of the great pioneer missionaries, Robert and Mary (Smith) Moffat. Livingstone's restless spirit soon rebelled at the tame routine of an established mission. Against the advice of their colleagues David and Mary set out on a long journey by oxcart into the unexplored territory to the north. They settled among a people who were virtually cut off from contact with the outside world by the wilderness around them.

Livingstone believed thoroughly in the civilizing influence of commerce as one of the normal, mutually beneficial forms of human relations. He saw that the material condition of the peoples could be bettered only by ending their isolation. So, after several exploratory trips with his family, Livingstone sent his ailing wife and children back to England and set out with a little band of Africans to open a road across the interior of lower Africa to the coast. First he went westward, coming out at Luanda on the coast of Angola. But the way was far too long and hazardous to be useful. So he retraced his steps and then worked his way down the Zambesi valley to the east coast. On the way he discovered Victoria Falls. For commercial purposes that route was equally disappointing. But his feat of crossing the whole width of Africa had made him famous, and he felt called to carry forward the work of exploration, so that others might more easily follow "with commerce and Christianity."

Earlier Livingstone had learned of the activities of the Arab slave dealers, for the trade with Arabia flourished unabated, and he had determined to combat it with all his strength. The rest of his life was devoted to opening Africa to legitimate trade as opposed to the slave trade.

Livingstone spent his last years, hampered by increasing illness, in exploring parts of East-Central Africa. When he died (May 1, 1873) his devoted African friends carried his body a thousand miles through hostile country to the coast. His ashes rest in Westminster Abbey.

The Opening of Central Africa

David Livingstone turned the eyes of the Western world toward Africa. The suppression of the internal slave trade and the opening of the continent became Europe's next order of business. Henry M. Stanley's tremendous journey (1874-1877) from Zanzibar across Africa to the mouth of the Congo River helped to open Central Africa to exploration and led to the founding of the Congo Free State. All the great powers of Western Europe became involved in a race for control of African territories. Ultimately a series of international conferences established basic treaties regulating colonial expansion and rule in the region.

Among the many agreements, the Treaty of Berlin (1885, reaffirmed in 1919) is noteworthy. It provided for freedom of trade and navigation in the Congo and Niger basins; repression of the slave trade and liquor traffic; rules for future occupation; guarantees of freedom of worship; and obligations that the signatories:

. . . shall, without distinction of creed or nation, protect and favour all religious, scientific, or charitable institutions, and undertakings created and organized for the above ends, or which aim at instructing the natives and bringing home to them the blessings of civilization.[1]

Stanley's journey also prompted the audacious plan of a chain of Christian missions right across the continent. This bold idea led to an unprecedented mobilization of staff and resources by many different societies over a long period of years, all with a common purpose in view. The strategic aim was to push rapidly inland rather than wait to become strongly established on the coast.

Ingenuity marked these early efforts. The upper Congo, for example, is navigable, but the lower river is blocked by rapids for 250 miles. So the mission boards had steamboats made in pieces small enough to be carried on men's heads and shoulders, which were then put together above the rapids. With these boats swift advance up the river and its tributaries was possible; and with one of them the British Baptist missionary explorer, George Grenfell, carried out surveys that enabled him to draw the basic navigation charts of the Congo River system. At the same time Anglican missionaries were pushing into Uganda from the east coast under the leadership of Bishop Alfred R. Tucker.

[1] *General Act of the Conference of Berlin,* February 26, 1885, Article VI. (See Buell. *The Native Problem in Africa,* Vol. II, p. 895.)

Mines and Plantations

Until late in the nineteenth century Africa produced hardly anything of commercial importance in world markets, so there was little scope for the development of trade. But the discovery of diamonds at Kimberley in 1867 and of gold in the Transvaal in 1886 changed the outlook. An era of spectacular growth began. Prospectors rushed in. Towns sprang up overnight. Railways pushed inward from the coast to the mining centers. Companies were formed, some of them destined to grow into financial giants such as de Beer's Consolidated, the British South African Company, and the Union Minière du Haut-Katanga. The recruiting of labor to work the mines began in earnest. The industrial revolution was under way in Africa with all its attendant dislocations and promise.

The central figure in this development was Cecil Rhodes, a man with energy to match his towering imagination, boldness to undertake the impossible, and a depth of conviction that overrode all opposition. In the end friction between the Boers, who again found their country overrun by unwanted outlanders, and the empire-builders led by Rhodes burst into open flame. The Boer War was the unhappy result and the scars of bitterness that it caused have never healed.

Plantation agriculture also invaded Africa. Planters in Natal began to grow sugar in 1849. To provide workers in the cane fields indentured laborers were brought from India from 1860 on. In the course of time the Asian community in southern and eastern Africa has grown to

14

half a million and they have gained a major interest in retail trade with their own distinct place in the stratified society of those areas. Today it is the Africans who supply the agricultural labor force whether in the sugar plantations of Natal, the sisal fields of Tanganyika, the oil-palm groves of Congo, or the rubber plantations of Liberia. However, in Ghana and Liberia especially, there are African plantation owners as well as workers, some of whom receive large incomes from rubber, cocoa, and other crops.

Africa in 1914

By 1914 the invasion of Africa was virtually complete. The map was well filled in; only odd corners here and there still remained to be explored. With few exceptions the peoples of Africa were in contact with Europeans.[1] Except for the newly-formed self-governing Union of South Africa and the republic of Liberia, all Africa south of the Sahara was parceled out in colonies ruled by one or another European power. The material wealth of the continent was being exploited by companies owned and directed in Europe.

Despite high-sounding talk about "the white man's burden" few Europeans had any interest in the Africans as *people*. To a great many government officials they were subjects to be dealt with en masse; to company officers they were "hands" to be put to work. King Albert of Belgium spoke with rare insight when he said, "The true

[1] "Europeans" is the general term used in Africa for all white people regardless of national origin.

wealth of Congo is its people." But it is doubtful whether even he perceived the latent capacities that those people actually possessed. More than anyone else the Christian missionaries were concerned with African people as people, came in closer contact with them, understood them better, and so learned to appreciate them more truly.

AFRICAN REACTIONS

How did Africans react to this invasion from overseas? Such a question was never put to them, of course, but what did it look like from the African viewpoint? To such questions there is no single inclusive answer. But there are several partial answers that shed light on the matter.

At first many Africans found it hard to believe the white men were real people like themselves. Visitors from Mars would hardly be stranger to us than were the Europeans, equipped with the marvels of advanced technology, to Africans living in a Bronze or Stone Age culture. An aged Christian teacher once told me how his father warned him when he was a boy never to let a white person touch him. "They are not people," said the father. "They are ghosts. That is why their skin is bleached white. They live under the water. I myself have been to the coast, and I have seen their ships rise slowly from the sea, first the sails and then the hull. They come with shiploads of cloth. And with the cloth they buy people to be their slaves. They take them, in their ships, down under the sea to weave more cloth for them. In the old days they took our bodies. Now they are more deadly—

they take only our souls. If you let them touch you they will take away your soul."

Of course closer contact soon convinced the Africans that the foreigners were people, but the cultural differences were still a barrier. New technical marvels—automobiles, airplanes, telephones, radio—ceased to elicit any surprise. *"Kindoki kia mindele,"* [1] "white man's magic," was the standard comment. "Everything he does is incomprehensible. Why should we be surprised at this?" Furthermore the African, too, had his magic, his secret lore, his language, his traditions and pride of race. He could outmatch the European in strength and endurance, in skill and daring in the hunt, in story-telling around the fire, in ability to wrest a living from unfriendly nature, and in contentment amid poverty. So why worry?

Obviously the presence of the European had its advantages. His medicines were powerful when illness struck. The magic of reading and writing was worth a struggle to acquire if one's head was not too hardened with age. In any case it was good for the young people to go to school and learn. Better tools and the skill to use them were desirable. Sewing machines and bicycles became tokens of wealth and sophistication. Most of all, the words of the Book of God brought comfort to the heart and opened the windows of the soul.

But other aspects of the white men's ways caused deep misgivings. The authority of colonial governments rested in many instances on treaties whereby the African chiefs or rulers accepted the overlordship of a head of state in

[1] Kikongo language.

Europe. Assuming that those agreements were made in good faith on both sides, it still may be argued that the African chiefs who made them neither knew what they were doing nor, in many instances, had the authority under tribal law to sign away the liberties of their people. In any case, it is a far cry from the tentative and limited control exercised by a colonial authority still unsure of its ground to the ramified interventions of a modern state into every phase of human activity. When the yoke of government rests heavily upon them, Africans recall, sometimes resentfully, the old days when such rule as there was lay in the hands of their own chiefs and notables.

Land has been an even deeper concern. Some lands the white man took by force, which is not easily forgotten. But even when land was acquired by treaty or by purchase, there was often a genuine misunderstanding on both sides. In old Africa outright ownership of land simply did not exist. The use of land could be assigned to an individual or a family, but all such rights were temporary and the land reverted eventually to the community. Research shows that all the land was held in trust by some communal body, whether it was used for planting or grazing, or only as hunting grounds. Under such a system no one, however great his authority, could validly sell the land itself. Therefore, from the African viewpoint, there is a flaw in all the deeds of sale by which aliens hold their lands. A great deal of the best land in Africa is in fact held by outsiders and in some territories Africans themselves are abandoning communal ownership in favor of individual freehold possession. But the feeling that they were tricked into parting with their ancestral birthright still persists and remains a source of tension between the races. Africans who have become cynical toward the European are fond of saying: "In our fathers' day the white man had the Bible and we had the land. Now we have the Bible and he has the land."

THE QUICKENING PACE OF DEVELOPMENT

Between World War I and World War II the pace of change and development quickened greatly, and new elements also appeared.

The Treaty of Versailles stripped Germany of her former African colonies (Tanganyika, the Cameroons, Togo, and Southwest Africa) and assigned them as mandates to other powers. The mandate system established three important principles for non-self-governing territories:

1. Administering powers were held accountable before an international body.
2. The welfare and development of the inhabitants was to take precedence over other interests.
3. The right of self-determination eventually was to apply in these areas, and administering powers were to prepare the inhabitants for self-government.

These ideas were no more than an application of the democratic principles that grew out of the French and American Revolutions. Yet for Africa they were revolutionary and many thought them completely unrealistic and visionary.

Little more than lip service was paid to the mandate principles at first, and the League of Nations itself gradually became too weak to exert much influence. But the leaven was at work in Africa as elsewhere. For the first time governments began to consider seriously their responsibilities in public health, education, and welfare. Eventually Africans began to receive appointments to responsible administrative posts in some areas. When World War II shook the political structure of the world it became clear that the mandate principles must henceforth become the cornerstones of governing policy. In the postwar settlement these principles were reaffirmed more explicitly in relation to the trust territories (the former mandates), and the right of the United Nations to receive reports on economic, social, and educational conditions in other non-self-governing territories was established. Political developments have continued at a quickened pace.

Communications in Africa have been revolutionized by the automobile and the airplane. A network of roads—still for the most part unpaved dirt tracks, but roads none the less—crisscrosses Africa in every direction. Motor trucks have solved the problem of local transport that a generation ago seemed insuperable. Furthermore the airplane has put all the major towns of Africa within a two-days' journey of Europe. Little crossroads shops are found everywhere, stocked with goods from the four corners of the world, just as in Europe or America. The barrier of distance has fallen. Personal contacts in every direction are multiplying. Planning and policy making can be done in full consultation, and in all parts of the world Africans are appearing and African voices are heard.

The period between the wars saw a great increase in capital investment in Africa. Industries multiplied and Africans began to qualify for an ever-growing range of skilled occupations. Today it is only where barriers of law or custom stand in the way that Africans are not found in the ranks of skilled labor. For example on the railway line from South Africa into Belgian Congo, a white crewman steps down and an African takes over, and the train goes on.

In the religious field the period since 1920 has marked tremendous change and growth. The important role of Christian missions in African education, health, and welfare will be dealt with in later chapters. These services have been one of the major formative influences shaping the new Africa. But the most important change during these years has been the shifting of primary emphasis from mission to church. A generation ago it was still, broadly speaking, the mission that made plans and decisions, and the missionary who took the lead in the work of the church. Today the African church generally acts through its own leaders with the missionaries in supporting rather than in leading roles. The African church is coming of age. This is happening none too soon, for times of testing surely lie ahead.

The church, and especially the personal influence of the millions of Christians in Africa, is already a powerful force, sometimes a decisive force in the life of the continent. Christians form a much larger percentage of the total population in Africa than in any part of Asia. But how strong the church will prove to be in the turbulent times before us no man can say. The historic movement we have sketched is still in process, still gathering force and momentum. The outcome lies in the unknown future. The churches and missions, the Christian people in Africa are not bystanders looking on at this many-sided struggle. They are part of it, and their whole lives are caught up in it. That is why this chapter has attempted to tell how it has *all* come about rather than following just those threads of the story that deal with mission and church.

From this backward look we may well take hope for the future, for in retrospect it is not hard to see Providence at work. We may be thankful that the influences that shaped the nineteenth century included the holy fire of the evangelical awakening as well as the birth of democracy and the industrial revolution. We may be thankful that God called missionaries to Africa throughout the formative years so that the gospel has been one of the influences at work, enabling the church to take form and gain strength across the years. Livingstone and his contemporaries could not by any stretch of the imagination have foreseen the Africa we know today. Yet their labors were used of God to prepare the Way in Africa.

CHAPTER TWO

Cultural Revolution and
Christian Mediation

ONE OF THE PERENNIAL FALLACIES THAT SHOULD HAVE BEEN laid to rest long ago is the notion of the "untutored savage"—the idea that so-called "primitive" people do not possess either intelligence or a culture. Culture embraces the whole gamut of knowledge, skills, and relationships by which people live together in an organized community, and in this sense no people is without a culture. Frequently peoples whom we unthinkingly call primitive are found to possess cultures of astonishing complexity and effectiveness.

AFRICAN CULTURE

Certainly this is true of Africans. To anyone who gets below the surface, the age-old pattern of African life is very much in evidence. A young missionary at the end of his first term remarked, "Now I understand the Old Testament much better than I ever did before." Even casual visitors are apt to see happenings that might have come right out of the Bible. The Hebrew shepherd lad has his counterpart in the African goat boy or cowherd. Saul sitting under a tree judging Israel is not far removed from the chief with his notables about him dispensing justice in the village square. The priests of Baal dancing in frenzy before their idols are close kin to the African exorcist with his "medicine" to ward off witchcraft. Women still carry water from the spring in gourds or earthen jars. People gather for neighborly fellowship in the cool of the evening and rise at dawn to go out to "bear the heat and burden of the day" in field and forest, or fishing with boat and net.

All this does not mean that African culture is derived from Biblical culture. Both are representatives of basically similar culture patterns that have been found throughout most of the world. It is our own highly elaborated technology, a growth of the last few centuries, which sets off modern Western culture from non-industrial societies such as are found in Africa. One observer has this to say about Africa:

Few Americans realize how rich and complex the cultures of many African societies were at the time of the first European contact. In the regions from which most of the American Negroes' ancestors were drawn, there were a series of strong and enduring kingdoms which deserved the name of civilizations on every count except that of literacy. In their arts and crafts these societies were little, if at all, inferior to medieval

24

Europeans, while, in the thoroughness of their political organization and the skill with which social institutions were utilized to lend stability to the political structure, they far exceeded anything in Europe prior to the 16th century. It is not too much to say that in their home territory the African Negroes have shown a genius for state-building unsurpassed by any other people, except possibly the Incas of Peru.[1]

Life in Community

In the vastness of the African continent there is room for great variety both in physical types and in ways of life. The aloof, nomadic Masai of the eastern highlands, subsisting on a diet of milk mixed with blood drawn from the veins of their living cattle, have little in common with the agricultural Kikuyu, skilled in craftsmanship and eager to learn, who live beside them. The slender, aristocratic Watutsi highlanders of Ruanda-Urundi show little kinship with the short, muscular fishing peoples of the upper Congo. The variations seem endless, yet they all repeat the same basic theme. That theme is *life in community;* a stable, well-ordered society in which each individual has his accepted place and function. From birth to death an African *belongs,* in the most literal sense, to his family, clan, and tribe. Apart from them he could not live. Hunting, farming, herding cattle, fishing—all are communal activities carried on together, never alone. With the group lies security, understanding, fellowship; outside, the danger and mystery of the unknown. Within the group one can talk and listen, un-

[1] Linton, Ralph. *The Tree of Culture.* New York: Alfred A. Knopf, Inc., 1955, p. 445. Used by permission.

derstand and be understood; outside are strangers of alien tongue and foreign ways who are not to be trusted. From the common life of the group comes the training every child and youth receives. Each accepts this training not for himself alone, but as a trustee responsible to the spirits of the ancestors for passing on the same heritage, unsullied and undiminished, to those who will come after.

Many are the devices by which this strong sense of community is sustained. Elaborate ceremonial rites, at birth, at puberty, at marriage, and after death, create ritual bonds between the individual, the age-group, the living community, and the ancestors. Secret societies serve the same ends. The multiplication of office holders surrounding a ruler reinforces the sense of participation and satisfies the yearning for prestige.

An African king's court may include a supreme judge, an army commander, a prime minister and cabinet, historians, interpreters, diviners, the heads of all the guilds —carvers, weavers, smiths, fishermen, boat-builders, hunters, and so on—and a host of lesser dignitaries.

Specialization pervades the whole of African life. "Few men can climb a palm tree, but everyone eats the fruit," says a proverb. Only men and boys may enter the cattle-pen. Only women may shape an earthen pot. Special guilds with special skills, trade secrets, and sometimes special magic, carry on all kinds of crafts, each of them serving the whole community. Thus the African community was able to exist, often with a reasonable degree of comfort, by the combined resources of its members and with little or no dependence on the outside world. In much the same way pioneer settlements of pre-revolutionary America must have lived largely by the skill, ingenuity, and mutual support of their own people. The "commonwealth" in those days was not a mere political term; it was literally the *common wealth,* the pooled human resources on which depended the commonweal—the security of everyone. In Africa this has still been largely true right down to this generation.

The Spiritual World

The life and health of the African community involves not only its visible elements and the common experience of its members. Even more deeply it involves the shared beliefs and common reaction to the mystery and danger of life. Rationalistic Western thought tries to explain the universe in terms of mathematical formulas. The African tends with equal readiness to explain all that happens in terms of living forces. His world is peopled with spirits. They are not necessarily good or bad; they are simply there, in the nature of things, expressing their manner of being by the way things behave. A sharp tool "has teeth," it "bites" the wood. A dish does not merely fall and break, it "jumps down and smashes itself." A useless, discarded article is "dead." A single tree on the plain is "sad" because it is alone; the dry earth "drinks" the rain. A motor car "sees" at night with its bright eyes; its motor "coughs" and "growls" when it wakes up, and sometimes the car "trembles with eagerness" to get going. These expressions are not merely picturesque turns of speech. To the African they are the obvious description of a world that is everywhere alive.

In such a world the most basic security lies in the power to control and manipulate these teeming life forces. Consequently the "medicine-man" was always a central figure in traditional African society.

Medicine men's activities were directed mainly toward the healing of disease. . . . To be a successful practitioner required a firm grasp of reality and superior intelligence. At the same time, the average medicine man was not a charlatan. He believed in his own powers and frequently possessed abilities in what is now called extra-sensory perception. He was also, in most cases, an excellent psychotherapist, and possessed a knowledge of genuine and quite non-magical remedies for common ailments. There can be no doubt that a study of [his] *materia medica* and healing practices would contribute significantly to our own medical knowledge. . . .

The medicine man must not be confused with the malevolent sorcerers, also found everywhere in Negro Africa. The sorcerer was . . . an all-round virulent enemy of the community, devoted to evil for its own sake. . . . It was quite possible to be a malevolent sorcerer without knowing it. Since all members of the community shared in these beliefs, persons who were detected and accused of sorcery by the medicine men would usually confess and submit to execution without protest.[1]

In such a society personal safety lay in being inconspicuous. The innovator, the non-conformist, in fact anyone who stood out from the crowd, was always in danger of death as an enemy of society. Change, unless brought about by external events threatening the very

[1] Linton, *op. cit.*, p. 430.

life of the community, could take place only as fast as the whole group was prepared to accept it. Life was much the same from one generation to another.

CULTURAL REVOLUTION

Beyond question there is a deep element of tragedy in the fact that this stable, quiescent way of life is no longer possible. The invasion of Africa put an end to the self-contained isolation of the peoples and communities. Village crafts are dying out—trade goods are cheaper and usually better. Store-cloth and sewing machines produce more abundant and more sophisticated clothing than skins, bark-cloth, and handlooms could provide. Bicycles shorten journeys and trucks carry produce to market at a fraction of the cost and effort of head porterage. No longer does the chief wield a power from which there is no appeal; he is a civil servant. He no longer leads the lion hunt, his job is to collect taxes.

The introduction of money as a medium of exchange produces a long chain of consequences, the most devastating being the fact that it puts man himself, as a wage earner selling his labor, on the same plane of value as the objects his wages will buy. In many African communities human labor is the only commodity that can be exchanged for money. Tens of thousands of young men go away to work. Their constant coming and going is one of the most upsetting influences in Africa, for they bring back into the local community a whole gamut of new ideas, habits, viewpoints, manners, and attitudes.

All this adds up to a process of social change so rapid

as to be revolutionary. In fact, when we reflect on the change in American society since our grandfathers' day, we realize that it has been as much as we could comfortably keep up with. Yet in the same period many African people have had to span the gap from Abraham to the twentieth century. This is "rapid social change" with a vengeance; it is a cultural revolution of shattering violence.

It is now time to consider the role of the missionary, the church, and the Christian school in this process of change. And to start, a few common misconceptions must be faced.

The Myth of Missionary Responsibility

The first misconception is the fallacious idea that this devastating change is all the fault of the missionary. A certain type of anthropology, largely outmoded, had its chief interest in cultures of the past and regarded any change as unmitigated loss. This school of thought tended rather naïvely to attribute all cultural breakdown to the influence of missions, disregarding all the other forces at work. Let it be made quite clear that even if no missionary had ever set foot in Africa the isolation of that past could not have continued. Inevitably the peoples of Africa would have been drawn into the stream of the world's life.

In fact the situation would probably have been far worse than it is. For the missionary has, in the main, been a mediating and constructive influence. On many occasions his presence and his testimony have ended abuses and mitigated human exploitation. Long before anyone else from the West was interested in African life, thought, or language, missionaries were living and working among the people and writing books that have become primary sources of African anthropology. Long before employers or governments were concerned with the African as anything more than "a hand," the missionaries were concerned with his mind and soul, building schools and founding churches, and helping the African to discover himself as a person and a child of God.

The Nostalgic Fallacy

A second misconception is that the past was better than the present. We are all prone to nostalgic longing for the past. Memory casts a rosy glow over "the good old days." So too in Africa. Yet however hard the present, few Africans would willingly live as their grandparents lived. The drugs, hospitals, and medical skills that save lives and restore health are as welcome in Africa as here; moreover, they not only relieve suffering but they reduce the fear of witchcraft as well. Automobiles and post offices, clothes and tools, newspapers and radios—new to African culture as they may be, no one would want to abolish them.

Basic Insecurity and Mistrust

A third misconception is related to the nature of earlier African culture. The seeming security of the cohesive old society was actually rooted in mistrust. There was no alternative but to sink oneself in the common life of the group with its give and take; yet one could never know

31

when some malignant force would strike. One's neighbor, one's closest friend might prove to be a sorcerer bent on bringing ruin to the community. In fact one could never know when he himself might become the agent of evil magic. Under the carefree surface of daily life lay a deep substratum of fear from which there could never be release.

John V. Taylor, an Anglican missionary who lived for months with the people of a Uganda village, writes as follows of the experience:

Sharing in the day to day life and concern of the people one comes to see many things from a new viewpoint. I was invited to celebration dances and funeral wakes, took my paddle with a crew of boatmen for a night's fishing on the lake, talked interminable politics with local Congress leaders and saw the grip of drink or magic upon individuals whom I knew as friends. People became real and lovable as I began to realize the daily life of the village in my blood and along my nerves. In such circumstances one is suddenly aware that one knows very intimately . . . how terrifying it is to be caught up on the tide of social breakdown. One learns what it is to take life as it comes without worry because no one looks very far ahead—but one also learns that the sentimental European dream of the happy uninhibited primitive is bogus because it takes no account of the deep mistrust of men with men which robs village life of so much joy.[1]

Clearly this mistrust that African society cannot overcome is a challenge to Christian faith. As Taylor comments: "Slowly there came to me . . . a new insight into

[1] Taylor, John V., in a report to the International Missionary Council. Department of Missionary Studies. Herrenalb, Germany, July 1956.

the meaning of the gospel and the nature of the church for the villagers of Uganda."

The World of New Ideas

Whatever one may feel about the old ways, the fact is inescapable that they are gone or rapidly going, never to return. To many people it is, as Taylor says, "terrifying to be caught up on the tide of social breakdown." To others, especially the young, it is the future rather than the past that beckons. This is illustrated by the comment recently made by a minister in South Africa:

As I move over the veld I watch how the herd boys spend their leisure hours. They still play much with clay, but what do I see them making? Oxen with humps on the shoulders? Sometimes yes! But what else do I see them fashion with their nimble fingers out of the damp clay—motor cars and airplanes. Out of the hands of boys there comes forth wisdom for men. The Twentieth Century already has cast its spell upon them—they are heading away from the traditional past and setting their faces toward a world of new ideas and new ideals, of new skills and daring new achievements.[1]

THE NEW AGE OF RAPID COMMUNICATION

All the processes of change have in fact taken on a new character within recent years because the world has been moving into an age of rapid communication. The power to send information more and more quickly from place to place, first by steamship and railway, then by telegram,

[1] Anderson, John, in *South African Outlook*, July 1, 1957, pp. 107-108. Used by permission.

telephone, radio and television has been one of the decisive influences of the modern age. The airplane, too, has made travel so rapid that distance is no longer a barrier.

There has not been time enough yet for any of us to have become fully adjusted to the change produced by rapid communication. It is easy to say "the world has become a neighborhood" without having learned the duties and privileges of world neighborliness. But this at least is clear: we are all exposed as never before to influences from other parts of the world. Africa is no exception. Any reason there might have been for believing that tribal peoples could remain tribal, or that dikes of isolation could prevail against the flood of change, exists no longer. We are all involved in a revolution together, and there is no way out but through it to a world fellowship. While it is easy to see and identify social breakdown, it is not so easy to see the healing process of growth and adjustment that is also taking place. The human spirit has great resilience; and in this respect the African is perhaps exceptionally well endowed. Africa's people will survive, and some kind of society will emerge from the present ferment, but whether it will be wholesome, happy, and free is still a question.

Missions and Communication

It is within the setting of the present communications revolution that the role of the Christian mission in Africa can best be understood. For communication is a basic aspect of the missionary's task. His first object is to proclaim the good news of Jesus Christ, that is, to communicate to others the transcendent reality which lies at the heart of his own faith, life, and purpose. Anything that prevents real communication is a barrier to be surmounted, an obstacle to be removed, whatever the difficulty or cost.

In this, as in so many other realms, we can see in retrospect that God has been working toward ends that were not evident at the beginning. In today's world the ability to communicate effectively with people everywhere has become a prime necessity, but no one could foresee such a development a century ago. Communication cannot be achieved at a moment's notice, however. It takes long and patient labor to overcome the barriers of language, cultural difference, and suspicion of foreigners. Missionaries were building bridges of communication with the peoples of Africa many years before the need was evident for any other reason than the proclamation of the gospel.

The Languages of Africa

The task of communication was and is arduous. The primary means is language; but Africa has hundreds of languages. Even today no one has counted them all or found a satisfactory way to classify them. In rough terms it may be said that from a line about five degrees north of the Equator to the southern tip of Africa the languages, with few exceptions, belong to the great Bantu family. (*Bantu* is the commonest word for "people" in these languages.) More than three hundred Bantu languages have been identified. Most of them are similar in grammar and vocabulary, but not mutually intelligible. West Africa contains several hundred other languages, roughly lumped together as Sudanic, though they differ greatly among themselves. Northeastern Africa contains still other language groups. Of all these hundreds of African tongues only Amharic, the major language of Ethiopia, had a system of writing and a body of literature before the modern era.

Even today, with the help of the work already done, mastering an African language is no light task. Most are tone languages in which slight changes of pitch or intonation distinguish different meanings. The structure is usually at least as complex as Latin. A typical Bantu language will have about ten classes of nouns in the singular and seven in the plural. These correspond roughly to genders. They are distinguished by different prefixes that are attached to related pronouns, adjectives, and verbs. The Bantu verb has an abundance of moods and tenses; but its special wealth is a bright array of suffixes each of which gives a new twist of meaning to the word. By this means a single basic word can be refashioned by a skilled speaker into scores of derived words, each with its own shade of meaning and its full range of grammatical forms.

Dictionaries and Bibles

African languages are often exceedingly rich in vocabulary. One of the few relatively complete dictionaries, Laman's Kikongo-French dictionary, represents twenty-five years of labor and gives the meanings of over seventy thousand Kikongo words; yet thousands of additional words are known to exist. Because of the stupendous task of becoming acquainted with the languages of Africa only a relatively small number of these languages have actually been thoroughly studied.

Missionaries have pioneered in providing African language Bibles, books, periodicals, and other materials. Some languages now have fairly extensive literatures, including the whole Bible or at least the New Testament. In many others provisional translations of one or more Gospels have been made, together with hymns, liturgical materials, and elementary school books. Printing presses and publishing houses have been set up all over the continent and an unending stream of printed matter in scores of languages pours forth. From 1928 to 1958 the International Committee on Christian Literature, with headquarters in London, supported this effort. Now, however, most of its functions are being transferred to Christian literature committees in the various countries of Africa. Important work is also being done in the field of adult literacy and in the training of African writers.

European Languages in Africa

The ancient barriers of the confusion of tongues are beginning to fall and it can now be said that almost any African can converse with someone, African or European, from outside his own community. From this time forward it may be expected that the most significant work on African languages will be done by African scholars rather than by Europeans. But this could not take place before Africans acquired competence in European languages.

There were definite limits to what the missionary could

express through the barrier of a tongue not his own and into a thought complex he could never fully enter. It was only as Africans learned the missionary's language and became able to share his thinking and feeling that the fullest communication could be achieved. At this deep level, drawing on both African and European languages, many of the most influential African Christian leaders are able to mediate new truth to their own people in a way no foreigner could ever do.

The Christian School

The chief organized means of cultural mediation has been the Christian school. Today the importance of education is widely recognized. Most governments in Africa give it a high priority, and Africans with secondary and university training are greatly in demand. It is hard now to realize what a bold pioneering step the establishment of schools really was. To a very great many people giving schooling to Africans seemed the height of folly. More than one group of missionaries entered Africa, even in quite recent times, firmly convinced that their sole task was the direct preaching of the gospel. To turn aside from that calling to build schools seemed to them completely wrong. Almost without exception such missionaries have changed their minds. Soul, mind, and body are not separate entities, of which one can be saved or helped without reference to the others. The gospel is addressed to the whole being. Godliness does not thrive on ignorance, but on understanding. Until one can read, the Scriptures remain sealed and the Christian is cut off from his most vital source of sustenance and renewal. Not only must the church have a trained clergy, its strength depends on an educated laity as well. The Christian school is the handmaid of the church. Furthermore, education helps dispel the fear of sorcery and magic, though new and more stubborn forms of superstition often appear where old ones are overcome.

For all these reasons mission schools came into being in ever increasing numbers. In some places almost every lad who completed the elementary course at the mission station became in turn a teacher, sharing with village children what little he had learned. Thus the basic tools of Western culture were planted in tens of thousands of villages all over Africa. Though many have lost their skill through disuse, there are some in almost every community who can read, whose minds are open to ideas and impressions from the outside world, and through whom these influences reach into the life of the group.

The values that Africans see in the Christian schools are well expressed in an address given on Fingo Day, May 14, 1957. Fingo Day commemorates a vow of loyalty made by the Fingo people of South Africa in 1835. The speaker said in part:

Your fathers included in their vow a special care for education—a truly remarkable thing when one recalls that they were what we would call today, with just a tinge of contempt, red blanketed heathen men.

What kind of education had these men of olden times in mind when they made their vow? Was it Fingo education? Did they intend that their children should be instructed in the knowledge that was already there—how to sharpen an *assegai;* how to make a good beer strainer; how to kill an ox in the proper sacrificial way, or how to scatter the bones upon the ground so that they had some meaning and some message?

Was it for the sake of such knowledge that the ancestors made their vow under the *mquashu* tree? If, so, what need was there for the ministers to start erecting costly buildings and to train and employ teachers in ever increasing numbers? The answer is simple. The initiation school offered adequate provision for the old ways. The new schools were dedicated to the new ways.

The education they vowed to advance was knowledge that had come to Africa from overseas; knowledge that had been born and tested in the Christian countries of the West; knowledge that could set men free from old fears; knowledge able to give men a key to the right understanding of the world they lived in; that could reveal new skills the mastering of which would bring men a place of new dignity and respect, and new ideals, giving birth to a new dynamic race.

Every nation's culture has its own profound values, and of such the old Fingo culture had its proper share. Even so, when a nation sees what will lift it higher, it feels impelled to claim that thing for itself, regardless of the fact that in the first instance this new rich pregnant thing must be mediated to them by men whose skins are white.[1]

CULTURE AND CHRISTIANITY

Missionaries not only have been exceedingly active in opening channels of communication but they have also been vitally concerned with the truth to be communicated. Christian missions in Africa have insisted that the door to knowledge should be wide open, *and* that the

[1] Anderson, *loc. cit.*

foundation of teaching should be the gospel of our Lord Jesus Christ so that knowledge would lead to discipleship.

The Gospel for All Mankind

This policy is essentially an act of faith. It presupposes that the Christian message is addressed equally to all mankind. The Christian world mission is based on a realization that the gospel is part of the universal human heritage. Man is not fully man without Christ.

The words of Scripture move the African as deeply and speak to his condition as directly as they do to anyone in the Western world. One old African woman, when she first heard the story of Christ, clapped her hands with joy and cried out: "I always knew there must be a God like that." In fact the African may hear the Word more readily and grasp Christian truth more deeply because his nature has been less cluttered and deformed by the false values of our over-elaborate way of living.

The Centrality of Christ

Distinctions must, of course, be made between the central message of the gospel and all the peripheral trappings of dogma, cult, and liturgy. This is not always easy to do. But there is no doubt that the heart of the gospel is Jesus Christ—

. . . who, though he was in the form of God, did not count equality with God a thing to be grasped, but emptied himself, taking the form of a servant, being born in the likeness of men. And being found in human form he humbled himself and became obedient unto death, even death on a cross.

41

Therefore God has highly exalted him and bestowed on him the name which is above every name, that at the name of Jesus every knee should bow, in heaven and on earth and under the earth, and every tongue confess that Jesus Christ is Lord, to the glory of God the Father. (Phil. 2:6-11.)

Wherever the gospel in its purity has been communicated and received, it has borne the "fruit of the Spirit," love, joy, peace, patience, kindness, goodness, faithfulness, gentleness, self-control.

People are people everywhere. Beneath differences of condition and culture is a more basic identity. We all have the same fears, the same hunger for more than material satisfactions. We are all so made that life lacks meaning as long as we remain bound up in ourselves. We find fulfilment in sharing and service to one another, in that unselfish mutual concern that the Christian calls "love." Yet in ourselves we are powerless to rise above our own selfishness. It is only as the love of Christ controls us that discipleship becomes possible and we discover the riches of fellowship and service "in the name of Christ." This experience, which defies every effort to reduce it to words, is shared by millions of people in every part of the world.

Church Life and African Forms of Expression

It is true, of course, that Christianity has been presented to Africa in Western garb. Not as an abstract principle has the gospel been communicated, but as a living spirit expressing itself through worship and song, doctrine and liturgy, sacrament and service, fellowship in the church, and the witness of courageous, temperate, unselfish living in the community. There has been too little time as yet for new forms, native to Africa, to develop. African music has been used experimentally in a few places and African art is beginning to find its way into the sanctuary. But the tendency to use existing patterns of worship and church life that bear the stamp of Western Christianity has thus far been stronger than the urge to express in new and African forms the ever-fresh mystery of communion with God.

Christian Community

One element of Western Christianity that has already been challenged in Africa and Asia is its excessive emphasis on the individual. Protestantism, especially, has stressed personal salvation, judgment, and moral responsibility—"the soul standing alone before God." This is not to say that in the West we are not all deeply influenced by the common life and standards of society. We are members of our group, our class, our nation, and consciously or unconsciously our group loyalties go far to shape our lives. But in Africa where the group is always more important than the individual this is even more true. The acceptance or rejection of the gospel has often been a group act. Masses of people have surged into the churches, most of them with only the most rudimentary understanding of the gospel and with little personal experience or conviction. Such movements present difficult pastoral problems. The task of conserving and deepening the spark of Christianity within these bodies of nominal

Christians, removed but one step from paganism, has taxed the church in every land and every age. African churches are struggling with it today, with varied measures of success.

Yet on the other hand this corporate unity and loyalty of the Christian group, however feebly Christian it may be, gives it an influence and a power of survival in African society. Current studies of the life of the church in Africa are shedding new light on the process of growth. This will be discussed in Chapter Six.

The New Community and the Old

To many Africans the appeal of the church lies in the fact that it is a living, growing fellowship that extends beyond the limits of village and tribe, and is able to endure while the old society is breaking up. The local congregation relates its members to a world-wide fellowship. Because the church speaks in the name of the God of all the earth, and because its message is attested by the Scriptures, it inspires a deeper faith than the ancestral gods. Christianity thus fills a real need in the lives of many Africans who are uprooted by the tides of change.

At the same time the gospel brings under judgment much of the fabric of African society. Many of the least defensible elements of the old culture have all but disappeared—tribal warfare, ritual murder, cannibalism, domestic slavery, and the wanton cruelty by which despots once satisfied their lust for power. In the realm of witchcraft and the fear of spirits, Christian faith wages a perpetual struggle with deeply ingrained beliefs. They will

44

not quickly be overcome; but it is important that Christianity should always be at hand to help those who find the old conceptions inadequate.

Christian Marriage and Family Life

It is in respect to family life, marriage customs, and polygamy that the church faces some of its most difficult problems. Throughout most of Africa in the past, and even today in some areas, a man's prestige grew as his wives increased in number. So did his wealth, since women did most of the work. A great man without a harem was unthinkable. Girls were married off at the earliest possible age, and unmarried women did not exist. On the other hand a young man could often find no wife at all without the help of older and wealthier kinsfolk. Marriage was the focus of many of the most elaborate ceremonies and social patterns of African life.

The Christian is not so much concerned with marriage as a rite performed by the church as with the whole life of the family, the way in which husband and wife love, honor, cherish, and help each other, and the kind of home they provide for their children. There are strong reasons for believing that the simultaneous polygamy of Africa is as destructive of home life as the "consecutive polygamy" of some many times married and divorced North Americans. Hence the churches in Africa have consistently maintained the ideal of monogamous marriage. But in the face of the prestige of polygamy, Christians are often under great tension between the old ways and the new. The churches also have perplexing problems in regard to the church admission of persons already involved in polygamous marriages. They have yet to make a place for unmarried women, or to provide superannuated ministers with social security to take the place of the simple device of marrying a young wife.

Tension Between Gospel and Culture

It would be a mistake to suppose that the missionary imposes his own answers to such baffling problems as these. Of course in the beginning he often had to say what he believed the gospel implied—not as missionary to convert but as a more experienced Christian to one new in the faith. But before long the African Christians themselves began to decide what rules of conduct would accord best with the new life to which they were called. Unhappily, rules have a way of hardening into precepts that are imposed on succeeding generations without the act of free consent by which they were first adopted. One is apt to feel that African church life is too legalistic, too much of a matter of obeying rules and too little a matter of the law of God's love written in the heart. This is perhaps an inevitable stage in the leavening of masses of uninstructed Christians who still "follow afar off" because they are not yet deeply touched by the gospel.

Yet one of the most hopeful aspects of African church life is that its leaders have a deep understanding of the tensions between African culture and the demands of the gospel. It is a subject of constant study and discussion in innumerable church groups. Ministers and laymen, rural and urban Christians of all the churches bring to bear their varying experience. In West Africa the Christian Council has held significant conferences on the problems of Christianity and African culture. Very able African Christian sociologists are helping the churches reach a deeper understanding of the issues. As Africans try to turn their own tradition to good account as a basis for a Christian society, they are like the householder in the parable of the kingdom, "who brings out of his treasure what is new and what is old."

CHAPTER THREE

The Impact of Industry and City Life

ALL OVER AFRICA STREAMS OF YOUNG PEOPLE ARE LEAVING
their villages and heading for the towns. This is the great
adventure of the day. Children dream of it; teen-agers
long for the day when they will be old enough to go.

In many parts of South Africa a year at the mines has
taken the place of tribal initiation rites as the ordeal of
admission to manhood. No other element so sharply
marks off the old Africa from the new as the existence of
the towns, plantations, and industrial centers and of the
people who live there. No other single experience
demands such a sweeping change in the pattern of life.
John Taylor has described this impact in a private report:

He whose activities have always been impulsive, dictated
by immediate need—planting when the rains fell, hunting
when game was near, building new houses when the village
moved on—now finds himself caught up into the world of

48

total work, summoned by the work-siren at the same hour every day, kept for a steady eight hours, every day or night, at a job which began before he arrived and which will never be completed.

These uprooted people present a major challenge to the churches, a challenge that is being faced and met with some degree of success. Yet there are aspects of industrial development—especially in relation to migratory labor—so bad that they are quite literally beyond remedy. Neither the church nor any other agency can cope with them as long as the causes that produce them are not removed. This is a task for Christian statesmanship in the largest sense.

THE GROWTH OF CITIES

Any visitor flying over Africa, as visitors usually do these days, soon becomes aware of the great cities set down, stark, new, and unexpected, upon the vast empty stretches of plain and forest. Only yesterday they were small towns, outposts of trade and government at points where road and river met or where caravans converged at a railhead, or where a sheltered harbor made landing possible on the coast. Today these small towns are big cities. Leopoldville in the Belgian Congo is fairly typical. It has doubled in size every eight years since 1926. It was then a town of 25,000. A half hour's walk from the center took one into the open country. Now it is a bustling metropolis of 400,000. It is too big to function as a single unit and is organizing itself into a cluster of cities each with its own industries, residential quarters, churches, schools, markets, and other amenities. Luanda, the capital of Angola, nestled for four hundred years between the ocean and the hills, under the shadow of the ancient fortress of St. George. Today Luanda has pushed up to the top of the hills and far out over the plateau and new streets are steadily being laid out and new communities built up.

In 1879 a pioneer missionary purchased from the local chief at Matadi a small plot of land, giving in payment "one windsor chair and one bale of cloth." Today the railway station stands on that land. Matadi is a busy Congo port, with houses rising tier on tier from the river's edge to the top of the ridge a thousand feet above, while whole hills have been blasted away to make room for docks and warehouses. Such instances could be cited all over Africa.

The visitor is also impressed by the vast plantations devoted to the production of rubber, cocoa, or bananas in West Africa, palm oil or cotton in the Congo, coffee in Angola, sugar in Natal, or sisal in Tanganyika. These, too, employ large numbers of men drawn from wide surrounding areas. They contribute to the movement of people that is so much a part of African life today.

CAUSE OF THE MOVEMENT OF PEOPLES

Why do people move about in such numbers? On the one hand they are drawn to the towns and work centers by promises of opportunity. On the other hand they are often seeking relief from village and tribal pressures. Sometimes this migrancy is no more than the adventurous spirit of youth, but if it is unsupported by some degree of training, skill, and aptitude at finding work the result is often bitter disillusionment.

Douala in French Cameroun is a city that keeps drawing more and more people in. Its paved streets, lighted at night, its stores, its markets, its schools make the city the inevitable center and home of progressive Africans. Young people especially go there to try their fortune with no idea what is in store for them. In the country young people are put upon. They lack independence and have no incentive. Life does not flourish there any more. In the country a man still belongs to his tribe. He vegetates in an old, closed economy, while life passes him by. We ourselves have been teaching discontent in our schools. Young people are torn between the bond of familiar ways—a tie that will draw them into tribal associations in the towns—and the desire to break away from customs that stifle personality. It is all too easy simply to condemn these city-bound young men without trying to understand what drives them. "We have escaped from death," said one of them.

But many of them find death waiting on the doorstep, for there is much misery in Douala. They put their hope in the city, they go to make their fortune, but unemployment catches them. . . . Only one man in five or six finds work. There are various odd jobs and small services which can bring in a few coppers to buy food. But only the blind or stony-hearted could fail to be moved by the cruel disappointment of the man from the country who sees all his hopes destroyed. The most desperate ones go back to the country, tired of knocking at closed doors, unable to sponge any longer on their relatives, and hungry.[1]

[1] Viennot, The Rev. Père, C.S. Sp. "Douala, ses problèmes d'Adaptation," in *Masses urbaines et missions*. Paris, France: Desclée de Brouwer et Cie, 1956, p. 72. Translated and used by permission.

Of course others fare better, especially those who leave the village with a work contract in their pocket assuring provision for their material needs. But time was, and well within living memory, when recruiting by force was openly practised. It was not uncommon to meet a group of labor recruits on the road, marching like prisoners under military guard, sometimes in chains to prevent their escape. Companies looked to government for their labor supply, and the authorities required each local headman to supply a number of recruits proportionate to the size of the village. Except possibly in a few backward areas such sights are no longer seen. Forced labor was repudiated by the International Forced Labor Convention of 1930 to which the colonial powers were signatories. In any case, the lure of steady wages and the attractions of city life generally assures a steady flow of workers without such compulsion.

Yet the big enterprises, especially the mining companies employing tens of thousands of workmen, must often go far afield in search of men. The *Union Minière* in southeastern Belgian Congo has pre-employment training centers in Ruanda-Urundi, six hundred miles to the north, and regularly flies its trainees and their families to the mining centers. Many of the recruits for the East African sisal plantations travel several hundred miles by sea. They also are encouraged to bring their wives, and the company provides a house for each family.

In other areas the situation is not so good. Thousands of young men go to work in the mines and plantations of South Africa, leaving their families behind them. Some come from the "Reserves," the rural areas set aside for African occupancy. These areas are often so crowded and so worn down by overgrazing and erosion that they can no longer provide even a meager living for all the people whose legal homes are there. They have become rural slums. For this reason a large proportion of the younger men and not a few women are compelled to go away to relieve the pressure and make a living.

Other migrants come from the protectorates of Bechuanaland, Basutoland, and Swaziland, tribal areas still administered by Great Britain, where conditions of livelihood are a little less rigorous. Still other come from Mozambique, Rhodesia, and even Angola, drawn by the lure of wage earning employment that they cannot find at home.

LIFE IN THE TOWNS

Anywhere in the world city life is primarily a question of income. People of means can be comfortable, the poor and destitute suffer. In the country, especially in warm climates, food can almost always be found and there is a tradition of neighborly helpfulness. In the cities even food has to be bought, and one may easily find himself alone, unknown, with no one to turn to. There is no loneliness more terrible than that of being a stranger in a big city.

The difference between the rich and the poor is very evident in African cities. With few exceptions the white people are wealthy by African standards. They have comfortable homes, automobiles, and servants. Heretofore their group has provided the managers, officials, professional men, and skilled technicians. Even where Africans begin to enter these classes, salary differentials often persist on the theory that the white man, as an "expatriate" living away from his own country, has extra expenses and is entitled to extra compensation. There are signs of change. Uniform salary scales regardless of race are making their appearance; and some Africans in business for themselves are now men of means.

Established African Families

The second economic level is made up of the established city dwelling African families living in homes that they either own or rent. (Asians also fall largely in this class.) These are the people who have found themselves; people with steady employment and fairly good incomes. They have learned the ways of the city, made it their home, and form the nucleus of the emerging urban community. It is among them that the city churches find their strongest members; it is through them that Christian social responsibility toward the less fortunate makes itself felt.

In many instances the people of this second economic level still think of themselves as belonging to the village and clan from which they or their parents came. It may still be a point of pride to maintain a house in the village, to be consulted on tribal matters, and to contribute to village betterment projects. The older ones may dream of retiring to the village when their working years are over. But more and more the city claims them for its own. Less and less, when choices must be made, are they apt to prefer the village to the city. As for their children, they know the city and its ways, but when they visit the village they are awkward and ill at ease. The village may have been the home of their parents, but it is not theirs.

This is true urbanization, a process not without some stress and loss, but basically necessary because it prepares people to live useful, happy, and meaningful lives in the new and larger world that is taking form so rapidly around them.

Marginal Workers

The third class in the new cities is the company "hands," unskilled laborers and others whose security vanishes whenever they lose their jobs. Great numbers of Africans live in quarters provided by their employers— a double insecurity for discharge means eviction. Low income coupled with inexperience in the use of money puts many of these people perpetually in debt, so they are seldom far from misery. Those who are fed and housed by their employers are materially better off while their work lasts, but they may be even less able to establish themselves when left to their own resources.

These marginal and sub-marginal urban dwellers populate the slums that spread like a blight around the more habitable parts of African cities. Poor people have no money to spend on houses. They "make do" with anything they can find. Many cities have failed to plan ahead in laying out streets and drainage—much less in providing water, lights, markets, parks, and playgrounds. The result is appalling.

The African house is very poor, with thin plank walls and a roof of mats. A few, better off, have greatly improved their houses; iron roofs are beginning to appear. This cuts down the danger of fire; there may not be any more fires like the one that consumed ninety-five houses and all their contents in fifteen minutes. The approaches to these houses are often so narrow one must turn sideways to get through. When it rains the passages become torrents. Sometimes one has to go through six or seven other houses to reach a family cut off by flooded streets. All this could be improved, but building is so costly and wages so low that few can even dream of it. A lot of houses never see sunshine except when the roof comes off for replacement. Alongside the houses are latrines, and eight or ten feet away a well. In theory this polluted water is not for drinking, but few of the children could deny using it. They are taught hygiene in school, but what can you do when there are only five faucets supplying clean water in a ward of 4,500 people. One faucet for 900 people.[1]

ENTRENCHED MIGRANCY

Such conditions are inexcusable, and the improvement of living conditions is a matter of high priority in most cities. Where Africans expect to remain in the city, and especially where they have some hope of owning their own home, they are often ready to work hard and sacrifice a great deal in response to help and encouragement from the authorities. A number of successful urban housing projects, differing in detail but similar in purpose, show this to be true.

[1] Viennot, *op. cit.*, p. 73.

The Impact of Industry and City Life

Contract Workers

All too often the migrants have no hope of remaining in the city, much less of having their families with them. Long ago the system of migratory labor came into use, especially in South Africa. Today it is entrenched not only in the habits of employers but in the law. Workers are recruited in the reserves or tribal areas for a contract period lasting perhaps eighteen months. If they are married they leave their wives and families behind them —in theory the labor recruits are bachelors. As a rule housing is provided. Often meals, recreational facilities, and health services are offered as well. At the end of the contract the men are expected to return home either to resume village life or at least to "rest" for six months before returning for another contract.

Initially this plan seemed to work fairly well. As long as the number of workers required was only a small fraction of the available supply the recruits were largely young men, bachelors in fact as well as in theory. They returned home, resumed their places in village and clan, and life went on much as before. The companies could house their men in dormitories, which are cheaper than houses. They could pay them single men's wages and rations with no allowances for wives or dependents. They did not have to provide for old age pensions or sickness benefits. Men unable to work were not rehired, they lived on in the village. When a mine was worked out the labor force could easily be taken elsewhere. Neither the company nor the city authorities had to worry about a lot of families settled in homes that could not easily be moved.

The South African government itself seems to have been glad to avoid the prospect of a large African population in the cities. On the assumption that Africans are only temporarily in an urban area for the convenience of their employers, a number of laws have been passed designed to control the permanent entry of Africans into the towns. For example, the Natives (Urban Areas) Act of 1923 made no provision at all for the settlement of African families in urban areas. This legal fiction still persists despite an actual African urban population running into the millions.

Lack of Normal Family Life

Of course the contract workers are not generally bachelors in fact. Many women also drift to the towns. When *all* the young men have left the village how else can a woman find a mate and fulfill the basic urge of her nature than by following them? When there is officially no provision for settled family life in the towns, the only alternative is temporary, irregular unions and such unions abound. In some cities of southern Africa it has been estimated that over 80 per cent of the children are born out of wedlock.

A recent social survey studied eighty-five households in Johannesburg. All had been established for fifteen years or longer, none were newcomers. Five households consisted of husband, wife and children, that is, normal families. The other eighty had no permanent male members. The head of each one was a woman who consorted with a succession of male "boarders" during their labor contracts, taking a new one when the one before went away. The girl children grew up knowing no way of life but this. The boys all ran away by the time they were eighteen. Some of them found work, others doubtless joined the gangs of young thugs, the *tsotsies* who terrorize the cities of the Union. The women eked out a living by brewing beer and by various other expedients.

Ironically, many of these people are regarded as sincere, earnest Christians. The life they live is not theirs by choice. It is the only life open to them within the accursed social system of which they are a part. A fir tree will grow tall and straight if it has a chance, but if it is thwarted by obstacles it will become stunted, gnarled, and grotesque. So it is with people.

Effect of Migrancy on Rural Life

The social corrosion of the cities spreads back into the tribal communities. Married men go away to work, leaving their families to their own devices. The village elders and the churches try to help, but the number of deserted families is too great. Some men send home part of their wages; many do not. Sooner or later a man takes another woman in the town. This is all the easier since in tribal society polygamy was not frowned on but carried prestige. However a wage earner cannot support several wives at a time, so he takes them in succession. By the time a man gets home from the mines he may be father to several broods of children. As long as he keeps going back to the mines any normal home life is clearly out of his reach. It is only when he is middle-aged and tired, ready to sit down in his village for good, that marriage can be considered. Then he may find a woman who, like himself, has lived in towns, and who has come back with her assorted children. It is couples such as these that present themselves for marriage in the churches. As long as migratory labor remains the basic pattern in mines and plantations, there is nothing the local churches can do to make things better. A missionary in Bechuanaland, the Rev. J. Reynecke, put it in these terms:

The Christian church in Bechuanaland has stopped trying to arouse any sense of moral concern about this custom. The whole tribe is nominally Christian—it followed its chief into the church back in the nineteenth century. Everybody knows that contract labor has brought the tribe down to a lower moral standard in matters of sex relations than it had in pagan days. But the men must go to the cities to work. What are they to do there? What are the women to do without them? How are they to have children and keep the tribe alive apart from the present customs?

So the church has adopted a completely legalistic procedure. When a woman has an illegitimate child she is denied access to Holy Communion for three months. For the second child it is six months, for the third child nine months, and so on. That is all, a routine sentence involving neither contrition nor amendment, with no moral or spiritual value whatever." [1]

Year by year the devastating effects of the migratory labor system become more evident. Even if the young people return to the villages they are changed. To them

[1] Carpenter, George W. *Africans on the Move.* New York: The Methodist Church. Women's Division of Christian Service, n.d., p. 12. Used by permission.

village life seems tame, dull, cramped, and poor. The migrant rarely settles comfortably back into the old ways. He is at least partly uprooted. Dissatisfied with the old, not yet at home with the new, he stands between two worlds with no security in either. Far worse is the situation of the children of migrants. Many of them have no ties with any tribal group. Legally they do not belong in the city, actually they know no other home. They grow up without parental control and without the discipline of tribal life. They have no principles nor moral values except "self." They are completely rootless—a lost generation. And as time goes on their numbers steadily increase, posing inevitable problems for church and community.

Signs of Change

Fortunately the whole system of migratory labor is coming under attack. It is still the dominant pattern in the gold and diamond mines of South Africa. But in the copper mines of Rhodesia the trend is toward a settled labor force, and in Belgian Congo this policy is fully accepted. In the long run unskilled labor is costly because it is unproductive. Migrants remain permanently in the unskilled class. There is neither incentive nor opportunity to advance when a job contract lasts only eighteen months. In South Africa and Rhodesia there is a class of semi-skilled white mine workers who fear that African advancement will endanger their own security. Through their unions they have opposed any change in the prevailing system.

But in Congo wartime shortages of skilled European

personnel added impetus to a movement already on foot for African advancement into skilled occupations. A stable labor force living permanently in the towns is being developed. Men already employed are promoted as far as they can go. Schools are provided for their children, especially vocational guidance and trade schools for boys and young men. As a result the companies have available an African labor supply of growing competence, while the Africans are assured of an opportunity to establish their families in the cities under favorable conditions. The steadily improving situation in Congo cities stands in sharp contrast to the deteriorating conditions in areas where uncontrolled migrancy is still the rule.

THE TASK OF THE CHURCHES

All these restless throngs, all these "sorts and conditions of men" form part of the parish within which the churches of Africa live and serve. They are the field of action of the churches; they also constitute its membership. They *are* the church. For the church is not something superimposed on Africa from the outside; it is the body of Africans, supplemented by missionary staff and resources, who are trying to fulfill the ministry of reconciliation that God has entrusted to them. What that ministry is, what can actually be done in each situation, varies according to circumstances. As already indicated the broad line of distinction falls between the migrants, whose world of security is being destroyed, and the more settled peoples who are re-establishing a community life under new conditions.

Service to Migrants

There are limits to what the church can do among migrants since it must so largely work *for* them rather than *with* them. Before they have been in one place long enough to get acquainted and become a part of the fellowship their time is up and they are gone. This is true both in the towns and in the rural communities from which they come. An itinerant pastor among the Ronga in Mozambique said:

I go into a village where there is a strong group of Christians to hold quarterly conference. We elect a slate of officers, and everyone is full of hope and zeal. Three months later I go back for the next quarterly conference, and what do I find? Not a single officer left! All have gone off somewhere to work. Then we have to start all over again, and next quarter, perhaps, it will be just the same.[1]

In the towns the task is harder because there is such a mixture of peoples, all speaking different languages, all strangers to one another. Churches and missions have tried, as far as they could, to follow their people to the industrial centers in order to keep in touch with them. This means that many churches have established themselves in each center forsaking the principle of comity whereby one church body undertakes the entire responsibility for witness and service in a given area. It means too that a pastor or church visitor has an impossible task in trying to keep in touch with a widely scattered and rapidly changing membership. To find the newcomers,

[1] Carpenter, *op. cit.*, p. 12.

to learn where help is needed, to bring relief where there is sickness and distress becomes a superhuman task when people are constantly coming and going and when language barriers break the community into a score of separate groups. Yet obstacles are overcome with unflagging courage.

At the very least, the churches do help the migrants to keep in touch with one another and with their families at home. Services of worship in a familiar language are the more meaningful when one is among strangers. The congregation is a fellowship drawn together by a common origin as well as a common faith, and able to stand together, to some extent at least, in the face of adversity. Many congregations regularly send back a share of their offerings to their home communities for the relief of the needy. This action is a symbol of the personal responsibility that the men *should* feel toward their own families in the village.

Furthermore the urban churches are an effective means of evangelism. People with idle time on their hands are glad to attend a gathering where their own language will be spoken. They hear the Word. Some believe and are baptized. A few become evangelists themselves and take the gospel back to their own people when they return home. In areas such as Mozambique, where the freedom of Protestant missions is limited, there are many villages in which the gospel has been preached and groups of disciples have come into being through the witness of men returning from the mines.

The churches and missions have also pioneered in welfare services and efforts to mitigate the misery and degradation of the human outcasts in the towns. Social centers, athletic clubs, nurseries, dispensaries, and welfare clinics have been provided, and there are Y.M.C.A.'s, Y.W.C.A.'s, and kindred organizations. Church leaders have taken the lead in persuading mine managers, industrialists, and corporate bodies, such as chambers of commerce, to concern themselves with the human needs of their employees. Missionaries and churchmen have drawn attention to subhuman standards of housing and hygiene, to indecent living conditions and bad administrative policies. They have served on housing boards, employment councils, and social agencies. They have promoted social research and have themselves done some of the best work in this field. They have tried to build bridges of understanding between the races, promoted acquaintance, mediated disputes. They have kept open doors of hope where otherwise there would be darkness.

Yet all that can be done to help migrant people is no more than a stopgap at best. As long as the contract labor system prevails its destructive effects will keep on spreading, steadily undermining the very foundations of African society. The avowed policy of the Union of South Africa is the "sound national development of the Bantu communities," involving among other things "the building up of a sound social order." [1] It is ironical that the Union

---

[1] *Summary of the Report of the Commission for the Socio-Economic Development of the Bantu Areas within the Union of South Africa* [Tomlinson Report], U.G. no. 61, 1955. Pretoria, So. Africa: Government Printing and Stationery Dept., 1955, p. 106. Used by permission.

remains one of the major strongholds of migratory labor, which more than anything else is destroying African society and making sound development of African communities impossible.

The Church in the City

The perspective of the church is quite different when it has a stable community in which to work. Not that there is less to do, but that so much more can be done. In any African city most of the people are recent arrivals with all the problems of adjustment that people moving to a city always face. In Africa these problems are greater because city life is outside the experience of former generations, and because the cultural cleavage between city and country is so sharp. The first task of the urban church is therefore to help people find themselves in the new environment.

Adjustment involves much more than the obvious needs such as getting a place to live, finding employment, learning to live on a set wage, finding out where and how to shop, becoming able to move about without getting lost, and learning a local language. All these are necessary, and the help of friends is essential. Members of city churches have unlimited opportunities for neighborliness.

But this is only the beginning. The basic need is to establish *a new community*. In the village everybody was bound together in an age old web of relationships. The city can only become a home when similar ties are re-established. No one fellowship, not even the church, can provide all of these ties. City people quickly sense the need to come together in many kinds of groups. They improvise a great variety of associations: for sport, for culture, for singing, for mutual aid, and for any number of other purposes. Many of these groups are fragile and short-lived. Many of them compete for support with resultant tension, friction, and disappointment. In the quest for community they are but broken reeds.

The church is able to provide a firmer foundation. For the settled town dweller, even more than for the migrant, it provides a genuine, living, lasting community. Within its total fellowship there is room for all kinds of sub-groups organized by language, by age, by interest, or by neighborhood. The church stands for all that is wholesome and helpful. It is concerned not with the trivial and superficial but with the depths of human need and the highest hopes of man. It builds on the home and family, and in turn reinforces them. It seeks out the failures, the wayward, and the lost, and wins them back. It prompts its members to care for the less fortunate and arouses concern for wholesome civic life.

Weakness of the Urban Church

Churches differ a great deal in their actual ability to do these things. Some are too narrow in outlook, too unaware of the ministry that might be theirs, too engrossed in routine to accomplish much. Many lack effective leadership. Urban ministers are often men transferred from rural posts, men who have had no experience in city churches and are themselves strangers to the life of the town. Few African ministers have had any specialized training for urban work, and very few city churches have either professional or volunteer workers trained for Sunday school teaching, youth work, and other types of Christian service. Church buildings are usually simple meeting halls without special facilities for religious education or social activities. Most urban churches in Africa have gone ahead, largely by instinct, doing as well as they could the tasks that come to hand, and some have pioneered in developing remarkably effective patterns of organization and service.

It is easier to do this when one church body is responsible for work in a whole urban community than when several churches, each with its own services, membership, and program, occupy the same field. In the latter case each church will have fewer resources of staff and lay leadership to spread over the whole community, and each will be in competition with the others for members and support. Yet it is sometimes possible, through a council of churches or similar body, to pool resources and plan together so that the churches reinforce one another to the strengthening of all. Almost every African city includes many language groups, and often these are served by different denominational bodies corresponding to the missions working in the areas from which the people have come. In some instances the rural churches have been willing to entrust their members to a church already established in the city, enabling the latter to develop a comprehensive witness and service to the whole community.

A Successful City Church Program

An instance of this is the Methodist work at Elisabethville, in the Belgian Congo. Here an interesting pattern of parish organization has been worked out to fit local needs. The whole city is divided into neighborhoods, in each of which there is a deacon and deaconess. They keep in touch with church members, teach inquirers, encourage family worship, and promote neighborliness. They are on the watch for newcomers and for people in need or distress. Each neighborhood group has weekly meetings either at the central church or in a local chapel.

There is also an interlocking organization of the whole membership on a language basis, each language group having its own chosen leaders. Since people come from very long distances to live in Elisabethville, scores of language groups exist in the church. Only a few languages can be used in public worship, but language groups meeting separately provide for a more intimate sharing of experience and nurture in the faith than would otherwise be possible. Moreover, language group leaders can give help and counsel in cases where the neighborhood visitors would lack understanding. Because of this more intimate contact, and because differences of tribal custom must be taken into account, questions of church order and discipline are often dealt with in the language groups. Only if some general question of principle is involved is a matter brought to the whole church board for review. This two-fold structure helps members to fit more quickly and easily into city life. The language group provides a circle of friends with similar customs and background. At the same time members are not limited to that small group, but through the neighborhood fellowship they are drawn into a wider circle both with opportunities to help others and with the assurance of friends close by in case of need.

Christian schools are no less important in the cities than in the villages. They are often supplemented by evening classes for working men, sewing classes for women, adult literacy courses, hygiene courses, prenatal and infant care clinics, and scout troops. These and many other undertakings are ways through which the church serves its members and the community at large. They are the more valuable because few secular agencies can provide them and because they meet the real and pressing needs of the people.

Finally, where the urban community includes several racial groups—Africans, Europeans, and perhaps Asians —the church is uniquely able to link them all together. But its record is not unspotted. Race prejudice has too often set up barriers that ought not to exist. Language differences and disparity of needs have been used to justify separation of congregations that would have enriched and strengthened each other. Even worse, European church bodies have been all too ready to "leave the Africans to the missionaries," with such support as might be forthcoming for that purpose, while their primary interest lay in extending the outreach of their denominations among the scattered outposts of

European settlement. All honor is due to those churches that have consistently kept their doors open to people of all races. It is noteworthy that when the government of South Africa attempted (in 1957) to impose segregation on the churches it was met with almost universal resistance. Many churches that had not faced the issue before reacted vigorously, showing that there was a genuine awakening of conscience on the matter.

THE LARGER CHRISTIAN RESPONSIBILITY

In all these things Africa is part of the larger whole that includes all people everywhere. African cities are much like cities anywhere else. African city churches have much to learn and something to teach through contact with Chicago or Detroit or Bombay or Singapore. African problems of race and industry will not be solved in isolation; they are part of world problems and must be faced as such. In this sense they are the responsibility of the whole church and of all Christians.

Seen in this light, it is clear that the church as a whole has resources that can be brought to bear to help Africa. Here are some of them:

FIRST. More can be done to help Africa in the field of study and social action. Industrialization and related social changes are taking place throughout the whole world. City churches everywhere are learning to cope with the tasks confronting them. A more thoroughgoing attempt to learn from one another, and to apply what is learned in one area to similar cases elsewhere, should result in gain to everyone. Already the World Council of Churches is engaged in a study of the "common Christian responsibility" in areas of rapid social change such as Africa, which should contribute to this interchange. And an in-service training center to be built in Northern Rhodesia will provide a good base for trying out new ideas.

SECOND. Future patterns of industrial development in Africa can be foreseen in advance, and plans can be made to avoid past mistakes and assure adequate provision for the well-being of the people involved. Power, especially hydro-electric power, is the index of industrial expansion. A half dozen major developments are either in process or in prospect, and each of them will clearly lead to a new industrial complex. Among such projects are the Owen Falls Dam at the outlet of Lake Victoria (completed in 1955), the Kariba Gorge Dam on the Zambezi (now under construction), the Volta River project in Ghana, and—much the greatest of all—the Inga development on the Congo River. In its first stage Inga will produce as much power as Grand Coulee. When fully developed it will be able to provide ten times as much. In each instance the churches of the surrounding area have taken note of the impending changes and have at least appointed committees to make plans. But much more could be done if the church at large would make available the needed staff and resources to help the local bodies go beyond preliminary discussion and into serious preparation for the future—especially the training of qualified leaders for Christian service in industrial areas.

THIRD. Churches must learn to cope with the "power structures" of modern society, whether these be economic interests, organized pressure groups, or established governments. It is not enough to deplore the destructive effects of migratory labor and other vicious practices, nor to try to meet them with feeble local remedies. Somewhere there are people who decide policies and who are able to change things. If better policies have been applied elsewhere and have proved their worth it should be possible to demonstrate them. If the mind-set of whole communities must be changed the task is harder and may take longer. But still it must be attempted because the consciences of Christian people cannot rest so long as evils persist that can be remedied. To do this involves more than local congregations, more even than national church bodies. It is a task to challenge the best minds and most sensitive consciences among Christians everywhere, a task in which the whole church must be engaged together.

Everywhere in the world the church faces this task of becoming "catalyst and conscience" to the new metropolitan areas with their complex structures of economic power and social control. A recent conference on urban life in the United States expressed it in the following terms:

The distance between what *the* church should do and what a minister could do was recognized as great. While a minister speaks to his congregation, *the* church must speak to the world. How does the minister play his role?

. . . In a way the conference was an answer in itself. Addressing the delegates on matters of racial integration, American economy, government and world affairs Bishop G. Bromley Oxnam personified *the* church speaking to the nation. The deaconess calling for more interest in meeting problems of hunger and poverty personified *the* church at work in the slums. The suburban minister bringing his laymen to recognize their obligation to the crowded inner city personified *the* church challenging the city to face its responsibilities. *Each local church member, each national figure, doing his part and recognizing it as part of the whole has his function as a member of the mystical Body of Christ.* The delegates were reminded that Jesus' ministry encountered its great test when he set his face to go to Jerusalem. The farmlands, the suburbs, the fine residential areas are not enough. The church must follow Jesus' example and set its face to go to the city.[1]

[1] Walker, E. Jerry, in *The Christian Century*, March 12, 1958, p. 320. Copyright 1958, Christian Century Foundation. Used by permission.

CHAPTER FOUR

Christianity, Race, and Nationalism—
the Patterns of Power

IN THE YEAR 1776 THOMAS JEFFERSON SET FORTH IN THE
Declaration of Independence the basic principle of
democracy: "Governments are instituted among men,
deriving their just powers from the consent of the
governed." At the end of World War I Woodrow Wilson
applied this same idea to minorities and subject peoples:

Peoples and provinces are not to be bartered about . . . as
if they were mere chattels and pawns in a game. . . . Peoples
may now be dominated and governed only by their own consent. Self-determination . . . is an imperative principle of
action, which statesmen will henceforth ignore at their peril.

But even in 1918 this principle of self-determination
was still ahead of its time. The great powers of Europe
ruled world embracing empires, and had no intention of

75

giving them up. Territories wrested from Germany were placed under the control of one or another of the victorious allies, on the ground that the dependent peoples were unable to govern themselves or secure their own advancement under the complex conditions of the modern world. It required a second world war to shake the foundations of the colonial system and make national self-determination the political force it is today.

Since World War II a score of new nations have come into being. They include nearly one-third of all the peoples of the world. But most of them are found in Asia and the Pacific. Africa is the last great area of the globe in which colonial patterns of power still prevail, although even as this is being written these patterns are changing.

Why has Africa lagged behind in political development? What is really happening now? To answer these questions it is necessary to look closely at two complex and mutually involved factors—race and nationalism.

RACE AND AFRICAN POLITICS

Almost everywhere in Africa the political structure is based on race. Seats in legislative councils are distributed on a racial basis, so many to the Europeans, so many to the Asians, and so many to the Africans, with the government itself appointing enough extra members to hold the balance of power. In South Africa, Africans may not sit in parliament at all but are represented by whites. In western Africa, where Africans are in control, racialism is found in reverse. Europeans are not permitted to own land or acquire citizenship. A white man is eligible for employment in government service only as long as no competent African is available to fill the same post.

This nervous emphasis on race is certainly not good for Africa because the special gifts of both the white and colored races are needed for wholesome growth and progress. However, it is not surprising that race looms large in people's thinking. It could hardly be otherwise in the light of past history.

The Assumption of Racial Superiority

When the European went into Africa he had no doubt whatever of his own superiority. He could not imagine anyone questioning it. Even though by the nineteenth century he was often animated with humanitarian zeal, his soul had been warped by four centuries of contact with slavery. If the Negro suffered under slavery, the white man was its victim in an even deeper sense for he lost the power to recognize human kinship beneath the mask of color.

You cannot enslave a man without reducing him, in your eyes, to something less than the full stature of manhood. The burden of guilt would be unbearable unless one rationalized it by saying: "Well, after all he is an inferior creature, designed by nature to serve." By the middle of the nineteenth century this rationalization of subjugation had so penetrated the subconscious mind of Western Europe and America that no other approach to Africa was possible than the one actually made, the carving of spheres of influence which gradually became colonies.[1]

[1] Carpenter, George W., in address at Springfield, Ohio, 1952.

Superficially there seemed to be no lack of evidence to support the idea of the racial inferiority of the Negro. Africans obviously differ from Europeans in body build and skin color. Their culture was also radically different and it was deficient in some important respects such as the art of writing. What could be easier than to assume that Africans were *by nature* inferior to Europeans? This assumption was accepted almost without question until well into the twentieth century. It is still current coin among uninformed and prejudiced people in North America no less than in Africa.

The Fallacy of Racial Inferiority

But racial inferiority can no longer be accepted as a fact. A long list of notable North Americans from Booker T. Washington to Ralph Bunche have demonstrated the capacity of Negroes to rise to eminence in many fields. African Negroes have mastered both the educational demands of Western schools and universities (where they often stand high in their classes) and the demands of political leadership in their own countries. Prime Minister Kwame Nkrumah of Ghana is a notable example. In other fields, such as music, dance, and sculpture, Africa has already enriched the world. Racial endowments may differ, but racial inferiority is a baseless myth. The scientific view is well stated by Linton:

In spite of numerous investigations and a great mass of literature on the subject, the existence of significant psychological differences between various races has never been proved. Apparently the members of any racial group can assume any culture in which they are reared, and we know that members of all the great racial stocks have made important additions to culture at one time or another. . . . Everything indicates that the differences which exist are *due to historic accident rather than to any innate qualities* of the groups in question.[1]

If African racial inferiority has no basis in fact, political patterns based upon it can hardly be justified today. Christians especially should be sensitive to their falsity, for equality of human rights and opportunities is a basic principle of Christian faith. God is the Creator and father of all mankind. "He has made of one blood all the peoples of the earth." The gospel of Jesus Christ is addressed to all mankind without distinction. In him there are not "Greek and Jew, circumcised and uncircumcised, barbarian, Scythian, slave, free man, but Christ is all, and in all." Christian bodies are therefore with increasing force and frequency demanding an end to political structures based on race. *People should count as persons and not as members of this or that racial group.*

NATION AND STATE IN AFRICA

Next to race, nationalism is the most potent political force in Africa. It is also a source of much confusion, for nationalism means many different things to different people.

A clear distinction must be made between a *nation* and a *state*. A nation is a people united by a common tradi-

[1] Linton, *op. cit.*, p. 28. Italics added.

tion, language, culture, and loyalty to one another. A state is a political unit exercising sovereignty within a certain territory, with one citizenship, one body of law, and one central authority. Several nations may form one state, as the English, Welsh, Scots, and part of the Irish *nations* constitute the *state* of Great Britain; or as the Flemish and Walloon nations constitute the state of Belgium. Contrariwise, nations may be cut by political frontiers so that parts of one nation lie in several states. This is the case with the German nation today, divided as it is between East and West Germany with substantial minorities in Poland and elsewhere.

One of the basic driving forces of political development is the urge for each nation to become one political unit or state, and for each state to become a nation. Thus the United States began as a federated group of small nations, the people of each colony sharing a fierce loyalty toward one another and a jealous dislike of the other colonies. But loyalty to the union has long transcended local loyalties. The United States is now a true nation-state, although local and sectional loyalties still move people very deeply.

Complications of State Building

State building is complicated by the problems of size and resources. Governments today are charged with many tasks that cost money. They must provide schools and colleges; roads, harbors, and bridges; public health; agricultural and forestry services; economic and financial controls; military and police forces; diplomatic and consular services; and missions at the United Nations, to name but a few. The more backward a country, the greater its need of the basic tools of development—capital funds, communications, schools and "know-how" —and the harder it is to provide them. Only a country having within its borders some resource that can easily be made to yield a profit can pay the cost of becoming a modern state. Only a state of substantial size can meet its running costs and maintain adequate technical services. In general, mines and factories yield surplus capital faster than farms, thus a country with a mixed economy is apt to develop faster than one that has to depend on agriculture alone.

These facts limit the application of the principle of self-determination, especially in Africa. In former days each tribe or "nation" (group of related tribes) in Africa was more or less independent and self-sustaining. But not even the largest of them is big enough to form a modern nation-state. There are hundreds of small tribes with no sense of loyalty toward any larger group, and although these peoples might prefer to remain separate, it is no longer possible. Political states are bound to grow and the public services they can provide are badly needed. African peoples must perforce learn new loyalties toward the nation-states that are now emerging.

If African governments are to "derive their just powers from the consent of the governed" the primary political problem of Africa is *to win that consent*. The peoples of Africa must be persuaded that their best hope lies in pooling their interests and their powers, in creating nation-states big enough to be strong. This must be, just as far as possible, a *voluntary choice,* for every attempt at coercion creates resistance and sets fresh barriers across the road toward the larger community.

The Example of Ghana

The new state of Ghana illustrates these problems. It contains six major peoples speaking six different languages. The most numerous people, the Ashanti, live in a zone running east and west across the middle of the country, and on into the Ivory Coast (French West Africa) on one side and Togo and Dahomey on the other. Thus the Ashanti find themselves torn between loyalty to their own past greatness as a people—a "nation"— and faith in the future greatness of the state of Ghana. To cast their lot with Ghana means acceptance of the permanent division of the Ashanti people by national frontiers.

The political leaders of Ghana therefore seek to dramatize the new state by every means that will capture the imagination of the people. Adulation of national leaders, flamboyant oratory, enthusiastic campaigning, intolerance toward minorities and dissident groups, vigorous promotion of public works and development schemes—these are devices that come naturally to young states seeking to deepen their people's patriotism. All of them have been seen in American history; all are found again today in Ghana, and will be found in other African states as they face the same crisis of loyalties. The very name "Ghana" recalls a legendary African empire which flourished centuries ago on the southern border of the Sahara. It matters not that there is no clear historic link between the ancient empire and the modern state; the name provides an aura of past glory for a state too young to have a history.

Nigeria and Liberia Struggle Toward Statehood

Nigeria, with over 32 million people, is the most populous country in Africa, but it is not finding the road to national unity an easy one because deep mutual suspicion between the peoples of the three regions makes them unwilling to become a unified state. The Muslim peoples of the north would have preferred to remain under British rule rather than become political partners of the more advanced and mainly Christian peoples of the south. During the constitutional convention of 1957 one observer remarked that "the Western Region wants immediate independence for itself; the Eastern Region wants it for everybody, the Northern Region for nobody." So a final solution will not be reached before 1960, though a large measure of self-rule is already in effect. Meanwhile people in all parts of the country are slowly beginning to think of themselves as Nigerians first and Haussa or Ibo or Yoruba second, rather than the other way around.

Liberia too has had its troubles in becoming a nation-state. The basic cleavage lay between the Americo-Liberians—the few thousand descendants of liberated slaves from America—on the one hand, and the tribal peoples of the interior on the other. The Americo-Liberians clung to the cultural traditions they brought from America. They spoke English, strongly tinctured with Africanisms; they maintained a representative government; they built American-style houses and lived as nearly as possible in the Western manner. For generations there was little real fellowship between them and the tribal peoples. Sometimes there was open hostility. But without each other neither could make much progress and the country remained backward. The first great change came when the Firestone rubber plantations brought employment to thousands of the tribesmen, greatly increasing the wealth of the country and also making it possible for ambitious Liberians to become successful planters of rubber. Subsequently the mining of iron ore added another source of revenue. In this new situation the Americo-Liberians and the tribal peoples have discovered how much they need each other for their mutual benefit. With the increased government revenues, roads are being built, schools are multiplying, and public health services are expanding. Old barriers between the peoples are falling and a sense of shared Liberian nationhood is beginning to prevail.

NATIONALISM AND DEPENDENCY

In the three situations just described there is a common fact: Ghana, Nigeria, and Liberia either are or soon will be free and independent states. Most of Africa is less fortunate. Its peoples are confronted either with a prospect of continuing in a dependent status or with the problems of a multi-racial society. In either case political development is made more difficult.

Christianity, Race, and Nationalism

British and French Colonial Attitudes

In preparing its West African colonies for independence Great Britain has taken a lead over the other colonial powers in Africa. An important factor has been the overseas training of thousands of young men and women, so that now Africans are ready to step into many posts formerly held by Europeans. The Protestant churches have also been a useful training ground in democratic leadership. The strength of the British Commonwealth is its voluntary character. There is no compulsion to remain within it. Consequently when a former British colony becomes a free nation it generally chooses to keep its link with Britain, as Ghana and Nigeria are doing.

The other major colonial powers in Africa have shown a less relaxed attitude. Nationalistic movements in French areas have been suppressed by force at times, and in some areas political agitation fomented by Communist-trained leaders has erupted into violence. However measures of home rule have been increased, and the constitutional plebiscite of 1958 offered the option of complete separation from France. Under this plan Guinea was the first to vote itself completely out of the Fifth Republic and Madagascar was the first to vote for independence in a commonwealth arrangement.

The Belgian Congo

Belgium realizes that within a few years she will be able to maintain her relation to Congo only if she is wanted as a partner, not by force. She is therefore striving to endow the Congo with a political system so well adapted to the needs and aspirations of the people that they will want no other. As a step in this direction each of the larger towns now has two burgomasters, one African and one Belgian. Belgium is also trying to establish such good relations between the races that the peoples of Congo will sincerely regard the Belgians as their friends. The many millions of francs spent in 1958 to enable Congolese to visit Belgium as guests of the International Exposition are a token of this policy of friendship.

Portuguese Policies

Portugal has in a sense gone farther than any other power in linking its African territories to the motherland. They are no longer regarded as colonies or dependencies; they are overseas provinces of Portugal itself. Africans who adopt the Portuguese language, culture, and mode of life are called *civilizados* and are eligible for acceptance into full Portuguese citizenship. Difference of race has hitherto involved no social stigma though massive immigration of Portuguese peasants into Angola is now creating tension. The avowed aim is to make Portuguese culture completely dominant, so that there will be one people with a common national heritage, living partly in Africa and partly in Europe. The political framework has already been set up—the *state* is one. It remains to make Africans and Portuguese consciously one *nation*. Unfortunately this aim leaves entirely out of account the existence of African cultures. Legally and practically the *civilizado* counts as a Portuguese; the rest of the Africans have no standing at all. This is the fatal weakness of the Portuguese plan. There is no evidence that the masses of the people will ever accept Portuguese culture in place of their own. The fact that only a few hundred Africans are admitted to *civilizado* status each year suggests that the authorities do not really want them to.

These patterns demand of the African an unusual kind of loyalty—a loyalty not primarily to his own folk and kindred, but to an adopted motherland in Europe, remote and far away. A few highly educated young people form this attachment, but for most people it is impossible or at best superficial. The result is tension and insecurity. People can only merge their inherited loyalties into patriotic attachment to a new nation-state when they genuinely feel that they belong within it and are part of it. Loyalty to their own people must be included in the larger loyalty. But if the state is felt to be the creation of foreigners, designed and run from overseas *without* the consent of the governed, then African nationalism is more apt to foster revolt than to engender loyalty.

POLITICAL DEVELOPMENT IN MULTI-RACIAL BRITISH AFRICA

The difficulties of political development in Africa increase from country to country as the proportion of non-Africans becomes greater. East Africa has more European settlers than West Africa. It also has a large number of Asians. It is farther from achieving nationhood because the mutual fears and jealousies of Africans, Asians, and

Europeans stand in the way. The three territories of Tanganyika, Kenya, and Uganda would make a fairly strong nation-state. Economically, federation would be advantageous. But Uganda aims to remain definitely an African country. It admits no European settlers and few Asians. So the people of Uganda refuse to consider any partnership with Kenya and Tanganyika.

Kenya has rich agricultural highlands where European settlement was encouraged after the railway to Uganda was built around 1900. The Kikuyu people had a valid claim to some of this land as part of their tribal heritage. On the other hand European farmers feared that African farms in their midst would introduce pests and animal diseases and endanger their prosperity, and that primitive African farming methods would result in erosion and soil destruction. This land issue was compounded with other grievances and was built up by skillful agitation until it culminated in the Mau Mau insurrection of 1952. Mau Mau leaders hoped to destroy all the white settlers, but a staunch minority of Kikuyu, including many Christians, refused to join Mau Mau. As a result the violence of the movement fell on them rather than on the Europeans. Thousands of Africans were killed by terrorists, but less than a hundred Europeans. After the first shock most of the Kikuyu reacted against this reversion to savagery, and the movement lost its force. But military action against the terrorists cost additional thousands of lives. Tens of thousands of suspected terrorists were placed under detention, and the process of rehabilitation has been a challenge to the churches as well as to government.

The result of this upheaval has been a determined effort to develop an interracial social and political structure in Kenya, and in Tanganyika as well. Ultra-conservative elements of all races oppose this trend. But the ability of some of the young African politicians is remarkable, and the right of all races to share in government is now admitted. This would have been unthinkable a few years ago. Redistribution of land, conservation of water for African farmers, and many other advances are under way. Partnership has become much more of a reality than ever before. Yet all of this is only a start. A few people in East Africa are beginning to see that the final goal must be a state in which government is not organized on racial lines, a state in which members of all the races feel that their common citizenship and common destiny make them one in a way that transcends racial and cultural differences.

The Federation of Rhodesia and Nyasaland was created (1953) in order to build a state with enough land, people, and resources to be reasonably strong. Southern Rhodesia has a fairly large white population, strongly influenced by the racist attitudes of the Union of South Africa. It has gold, coal, chrome and asbestos mines, factories, skilled labor, and capital. Northern Rhodesia is rich in copper but thinly peopled. Nyasaland exports manpower, especially to the copper mines, but produces little else. Economically the three territories reinforce one another. But the African populations in Northern Rhodesia and Nyasaland oppose federation because they fear domination by Southern Rhodesia. The professed aim of the federation is racial partnership, but this has not thus far been defined or worked out in ways that would reassure the Africans. The one political leader who had the confidence of large numbers of Africans as well as Europeans, R. S. Garfield Todd (a former missionary) was forced out of office as prime minister of Southern Rhodesia by those who felt he was too outspoken an advocate of African advance. The destiny of the Federation hangs in the balance.

CRISIS IN SOUTH AFRICA

All the issues of state building are met in their sharpest form in the Union of South Africa. In fact the basic question in the Union today is not *how* to unite several nations into one state. Its people are divided over the question whether such a union should be permitted at all.

To understand South Africa it is necessary to take account of the mixture of peoples who live there. The population of the Union is made up roughly as follows:

    9,500,000 Africans (including four major ethnic
              groups)
    3,000,000 Europeans (60 per cent Afrikaans speak-
              ing, 40 per cent English speaking)
    1,300,000 Colored (of mixed ancestry)
      400,000 Asians

The Europeans, though a minority, have developed an industrial civilization and a cultural tradition on a par with those of the West. They are determined not to be "engulfed" by the overwhelming numbers of Africans who live in South Africa in a very different cultural tradition.

The English speaking South Africans, imbued with liberal traditions, foresaw a gradual emergence of Africans and "colored" peoples into the European pattern of life. The franchise was extended to those who met certain qualifications. The leveling-up process was slow, but it was unmistakable; the doors were open to Africans who chose to adopt European culture. Until 1948, when the Afrikaners' Nationalist party came to power, this was the dominant political philosophy of South Africa, however hesitantly applied in practice.

All this was abhorrent to the Afrikaner. He believed in domination. He had no use for racial equality or other liberal ideas. Back in the early nineteenth century a quarrel with the British over the abolition of slavery gave rise to the Great Trek (1835-1837) in which several thousand Afrikaners moved into the northern wilderness. On the way they fought wars with the Zulu, Matabele, and other tribes, of whom many were afterwards impressed into service on Afrikaner farms. The Great Trek marks the rise of the Afrikaner nation, conscious of its peculiar destiny and imbued with a deeply religious sense of vocation. All that the Old Testament says about Israel as God's chosen people the Afrikaner applies to himself.

Out of the harsh world of rock and stone they had come to the grass country, all green and smiling . . . and as God had chosen them for a people, so did they choose him for their God, cherishing their separateness that was now his will. They set their conquered enemies apart, ruling them with unsmiling justice.[1]

The special calling of the Afrikaner nation has been a favorite theme of generations of preachers in their churches. Implicit in it is authority over "the people of the land" but also paternal responsibility for them. The Dutch Reformed Churches support an impressive missionary work, and the social welfare program of the Nationalist Party goes far beyond anything previously attempted. But Afrikaner freedom (implying domination over others) remains the basic principle.

The ideal of the Voortrekker was a piece of land so large that when he sat smoking his pipe on the stoop of his farmhouse he would not see the smoke rising from the chimney of the neighboring farmhouse. That did not mean a desire to possess lots of land, but a desire for freedom.[2]

But freedom through isolation could not be maintained. The discovery of diamonds in 1867 and gold in 1886 brought hordes of "outlanders" into the north, turned farms into camps and cities, and resulted in the Boer War (1899-1902). More recently the growth of industry has been draining African labor from the farms, raising wages, and destroying the old master-servant relationship. The cultural isolation of the farmer is ended. Afrikaners themselves are entering industry and becoming city-dwellers in increasing numbers.

[1] Paton, Alan. *Too Late the Phalarope.* N.Y.: Charles Scribners Sons, 1953, p. 17. Used by permission.
[2] Buskes, J. J. *South Africa's Apartheid Policy—Unacceptable,* translated by Dr. Arthur W. Blaxall. Johannesburg, So. Africa. p. 14. Privately circulated.

The Doctrine of Apartheid

In 1948 an unexpected political victory brought the Nationalist Party into power. The new government began at once a systematic attempt to enforce its concept of apartheid, or separate development on racial lines.[1] For all its roots in the past apartheid was to some extent an instinctive reaction rather than a carefully thought-out system. It was an attempt to set right everything that seemed, from the Nationalist viewpoint, to have gone wrong under "the careless British laissez-faire regime" of previous governments.

A long series of increasingly harsh measures marks the application of apartheid. Under the Group Areas Act, Africans and Asians are being dispossessed of homes and businesses in "white areas" with little compensation. The Suppression of Communism Act enables the government to silence almost any outspoken critic as a "statutory Communist." The Mixed Marriages Act forbids marriages between members of different racial groups. Its enforcement is resulting in the separation of many families without regard to what happens to the children. The Bantu Education Act took almost all education away from churches and missions on the pretext of putting the schools under community control. It made teacher training a government monopoly. The real aim was to impose on Africans an education that would not encourage them

---

[1] A dictionary definition of apartheid is "separation of the races; specifically in South Africa a policy of segregation and political and economic discrimination. . . ."

to "seek to penetrate the white man's society or to participate in the latter's government." The Native Laws Amendment Act empowered the government, under certain conditions, to prohibit interracial gatherings. With remarkable force and unanimity the churches (except the Dutch Reformed churches) have declared their intention to defy this act should it be implemented.

It is increasingly clear that the "ideal" apartheid of theory can never be realized in practice. Apartheid, as defined and supported by the Dutch Reformed churches, would provide opportunities for separate development and local self-government with a measure of freedom and justice for all groups.

But "ideal" apartheid is still a dream. It would require complete territorial separation, which Dr. Daniel Malan, when he was Prime Minister, categorically declared to be impossible. It would deprive industry and the mines of the African labor supply on which the whole economy of the country depends. It would require an expenditure of at least two hundred million dollars on the development of Bantu areas, toward which only token grants have been made thus far.

Even Afrikaners are beginning to question apartheid, but they have no alternative to suggest. Stripped of abstract theory it has proved in practice to be nothing more than a last-ditch effort to defend the status quo by repressive measures. But it is impossible to turn the clock back. The basic conflict of group aspirations remains.

On the part of the European population there is an unshakable resolve to maintain their right of self-determination as a national and racial entity; while on the part of the Bantu there is a growing conviction that they are entitled to . . . the fruits of integration, including an ever greater share in the control of the country.[1]

The result is steadily mounting tensions with no prospect of relief. Both within the Union of South Africa and in the world outside an increasing number of people would concur in the judgment expressed by the well-known South African author, Alan Paton:

> If the white South Africans, in whose hands rests the power of decision, do not choose while there is time to reverse the present trend and to begin the building of one South African nation-state, open to all, they cannot indefinitely maintain white supremacy by force. In the end this may well be changed into black supremacy by rebellion and violence.[2]

THE ROLE OF THE CHURCHES

In all these situations in various parts of Africa the churches and their members are deeply involved. In fact the church often bears within itself the tension between opposing viewpoints.

On the one hand Christianity has entered Africa hand-in-hand with Western culture. The colonial powers are all ostensibly Christian nations. The more constructive aspects of colonial development have been aided and often guided by Christian missions. Governments in turn have subsidized the educational and medical work of missions and sometimes even supported their religious activities. A large proportion of the Europeans living in Africa are

[1] [Tomlinson Report]: *op. cit.*, p. 105.
[2] Alan Paton, in conversation with author.

themselves Christians and regard the church as a constructive and stabilizing influence.

Africans, too, claim Christianity for their own. Millions of Africans have become Christians. They find in the gospel not only their truest ideals but also the basis of their claim to justice, freedom, and equality.

. . . If God is no respecter of persons, why should any man be? If men and women are created by God and loved equally by Him, then women must be allowed education and a fuller participation in the total life of society. If there is neither Jew nor Greek in God's presence, then the colonial ruler has no more right to rule the colonial than the colonial has to rule him . . .[1]

If the church had the brittleness of a man made institution it might be torn in pieces by this conflict. But in fact this tension within the church and within Christian people can be creative. It releases the power of God into the world of men for the accomplishment of his redemptive purpose. Deeply as the church may be involved in situations where entrenched privilege gives the lie to the gospel, Christians are still under orders: "Do not be conformed to this world but be transformed by the renewal of your mind, that you may prove what is the will of God, what is good and acceptable and perfect." Sometimes the church responds corporately; sometimes, in various ways, individual Christians and small groups bear faithful witness in the face of overwhelming odds. Both are significant.

[1] Karefa-Smart, Rena. "Africa Asks Questions of the West," *The Ecumenical Review,* October 1957, p. 53. Used by permission.

Corporate Witness

In Africa as elsewhere local congregations are integrated in denominational bodies, and many of these church and mission bodies are united in national Christian councils. Beyond these are the world bodies, the International Missionary Council linking the Christian councils together, and the World Council of Churches linking many of the churches. One of the tasks of the national Christian councils is to provide a channel of communication between the churches and government. A great variety of questions are dealt with in this way, from local problems through questions of public welfare, education, and morals to basic issues of human rights and national policy.

At moments of crisis the moderating influence of the churches is often great. In Kenya it was the churches that saved the country from mass reprisals against the Kikuyu after the Mau Mau violence. In South Africa leaders of the churches were among those who established a Treason Trials Defense Fund on behalf of the 156 persons of all races rounded up in a politically-inspired mass arrest. The vigilance of the churches is a valuable safeguard of minority rights.

Reconciliation

Often the churches, or groups animated by Christian concern, are in a position to mediate opposing viewpoints. The South African Institute of Race Relations has striven through the years to promote understanding across racial lines. Wilgespruit Fellowship Center near Johannesburg encourages personal acquaintance and fellowship regardless of race. Multi-racial study groups in Kenya prepared the ground for political advance. Some of the churches are themselves interracial bodies. All of them are representatives of a fellowship that transcends race and culture. Within that fellowship, and under the compulsion of the love of God, differences can be overcome and common ground explored together. "The ministry of reconciliation" is the special calling of the church.

Prophetic Voices

Even in the midst of crisis the Spirit of God prompts courageous individuals to speak out in protest against injustice, declaring the judgment of God on human wrongdoing. A notable instance is the strong criticism of apartheid by B. B. Keet a professor of Stellenbosch University. As he is himself an eminent theologian of the Dutch Reformed Church, his words carry weight. The following passage is condensed from a lecture on "The Ethics of Apartheid."

In our South African situation we have all the injustices of group-thinking aggravated by absurd group-formation according to the color of one's skin. We have developed a caste system which surpasses all others, for there is no possibility of change—the colored man stays colored even if he is a most exemplary citizen. He is a mere cipher without personal attributes or claims.

Halford E. Luccock tells of a census-taker who called at a flat in a crowded American city. A woman came to the door with four or five children clinging to her. He asked: "How

98

many children have you?" The woman answered: "Well, let's see. There's Agatha and Jonathan and Cleopatra . . ." "Never mind the names, give me the number." The woman drew up to the full height of her dignity and said: "In our family, sir, children have no numbers, they have names." Is not that the core of the Christian ethic which must be proclaimed in this increasingly impersonal world?

We must abandon the habit of group thinking which ignores the individual because of his color. Color prejudice is the greatest single cause of black nationalism. Widely divergent groups are being driven together to form a solid front hostile to the whites.

Apartheid takes the less advanced individuals as normative of the whole. It reverses the trend of Western civilization toward a casteless society in which not even the meanest is an outcast but everyone feels himself part of the nation.

It is suicidal for the Europeans in South Africa to adhere to these artificial color divisions. Along these lines the prospects for the survival of white South Africa are bleak indeed.[1]

Incitement to Creative Action

Christian concern sometimes leads individuals and small groups of people to break through the walls of convention in search of new and daring solutions to the problems that vex them. In South Africa where neither of the major political parties had any positive program for interracial co-operation a group of people, among whom Alan Paton is the most widely known, have boldly formed a Liberal Party. The very word "liberal" is abhorrent to Afrikaner ears, and many Africans and Asians have become too disillusioned to trust any white man. So the

[1] Keet, B. B. *The Ethics of Apartheid*, pp. 18-20. Used by permission.

party is small in numbers, but its influence is considerable, for its very existence compels the major parties to face the issues of racial injustice.

In the Rhodesias and East Africa the Capricorn Africa Society serves a similar purpose. This society "takes its stand on the dignity and worth of the human person as such and acknowledges no right to power except the capacity to serve." [1] By a long process of discussion in multiracial citizenship committees, a Capricorn charter defining the principles of "an interracial, integrated society" was drafted. This was adopted at a great out-of-doors conference at Salima, Nyasaland, in September 1956. Since then it has been the aim of the society to foster movements in each country to get the principles of the charter written into law. To this end it is promoting "schools of citizenship" in Southern Rhodesia and Kenya.

The motivation of the Capricorn movement is Christian. Its founder is Colonel David Stirling, a devout Roman Catholic, who was a famous commando during World War II. But such a movement must have room for people of many faiths. As Col. Stirling puts it: "For myself, Capricorn is the political expression of my deepest religious convictions. I hope the same may be true for my Asian and African friends, whatever their faith."

Social Reconstruction

Political development depends on a healthy society. The role of the churches in strengthening urban commu-

[1] Oldham, J. H. *New Hope in Africa.* N. Y.: Longmans Green and Co., Inc., 1955, p. 15. Used by permission.

nity life, described in Chapter Three, is an indirect contribution to political advance. After the Mau Mau crisis in Kenya the churches led the way in service under very difficult conditions. More than seventy thousand Africans suspected of terrorism were in detention camps, members of the same family often widely separated. In the cities Africans lived in compounds surrounded with barbed wire and guarded against attacks by terrorists still at large. Fear and hatred poisoned relations between the races. Reconciliation seemed impossible.

But the churches were not dismayed. Under the leadership of the Secretary of the Christian Council of Kenya, the late Dr. Stanley A. Morrison, rehabilitation was begun. Chaplains and welfare officers were provided for the camps. In revulsion from Mau Mau thousands of people experienced a change of heart and found new life in Christ.

As detainees were placed on parole in labor camps, Christian workers brought teaching and guidance. Rural Kikuyu were gathered from isolated homesteads into villages. For them this was a new pattern of life. Christian village leaders helped them learn how to live together. In the cities new Christian centers provided fellowship and service. Personnel and financial help were provided by the World Council of Churches, the British Council of Churches, and Church World Service. The results have been remarkable.

Thus in many ways, by witness and service, the church and its members sustain the peoples of Africa in their efforts to find a more abundant life through political development. The way is long, the obstacles are many. Clearly the greatest obstacle of all is the sinful human preference for the seeming security of the small closed circle of intimates that denies the larger claims of the whole family of man. By its very nature the gospel sets itself to overcome that obstacle, making of the many "one new man in Christ."

CHAPTER FIVE

Which Way, Young Africa?

WHEN DAVID LIVINGSTONE'S CARRIERS FIRST CAME IN SIGHT of the ocean at Luanda they exclaimed: "Our fathers have always said the land was endless; but now, see! The land is saying to us, 'I am finished. There is no more of me.'" That was in 1854. Now, a century later, it is not only a handful of young men in Africa whose familiar ways are suddenly at an end; as we stand at the edge of the age of space we are all there with them facing the new and the unknown. All the well-known landmarks of experience lie behind us.

The most that we dare to say about the future is that it will surely not be like the past. When we discuss Africa's search for ethical and spiritual guidance we must recognize that we are involved in the same search. If we or they fail to find the road, we all shall be lost with the same lostness.

103

THE BROKENNESS OF THE MODERN WORLD

The tragic state of the world is symbolized by the fact that inconceivable power now lies in human hands and threatens the annihilation of life itself. The nations most advanced in technology, whose people are historically within the Christian tradition and who as peoples have no animosity toward one another, are frantically building up arsenals of destruction, which, as everyone knows, it would be fatal folly to use. Every sensitive person is torn by a deep inner tension that reflects the conflict between belief and action.

The more we grow in essential solidarity with Christ, the greater is our discontent with . . . the disunited world in which we live—a disunity now made all the more vivid by the fearful competition in man's penetration of outer space. The plain truth is that ours is a tragically broken world. This brokenness infects the church's life and work. . . . As Christians we are deeply enmeshed in that which we deplore.

It is hard to be human in today's broken world. Pressured, overstimulated, pulled this way or that by competing loyalties, fragmented by his varied roles and functions, menaced by the constant threat of war, contemporary man appears sometimes to be less than human. These hazards are increased by a society in which sheer bigness, rapid change, and the loss of control over the very means of control which scientific ingenuity has devised spell ambiguity and spiritual despair.[1]

[1] National Council of Churches. Message of Fourth General Assembly, 1957.

104

Yet even within the setting of this general brokenness Africa has a special brokenness of its own. We at least have a point of reference, a period of relative stability in the past during which there was a gradual building up of experience in the use of technology. Christianity was part of our heritage, and the moral standards of prophetic religion are reasonably well known even if not adequately practiced. Africa does not have these advantages. The young people of Africa have never in their lives had a clear, straight road to follow. Perplexities and confusions are their daily experience. Even the various kinds of nationalism that seek their allegience are clearly becoming outmoded before they are attained. Today nation-states must unite in supra-national blocs to match the strength of other blocs in the giant politics now emerging throughout the world. Many Africans would certainly join in the lament voiced in the following poem by Mabel Jolaoso of West Africa:

> Here we stand
> Infants overblown,
> Poised between two civilizations,
> Finding the balance irksome,
> Itching for something to happen
> To tip us one way or the other,
> Groping in the dark for a helping hand—
> And finding none.
> I'm tired. O my God, I'm tired,
> I'm tired of hanging in the middle way—
> But where can I go? [1]

[1] Jolaoso, Mabel Imonkhude. "Conflict," published in the magazine, *Odu*. Nigeria, 1956.

Cross-cultural Contradictions

Young Africans, like other people, want to do what is right and to win approval. But how can one decide what is right when he is pulled two ways at once by different culture patterns?

For instance, a young man takes a position as shop-keeper in a village. In terms of European culture he is entrusted with a trading stock, and is accountable to the owner for its value. But in some tribes, by a tradition that comes down from the time when money was still un-known, it is a point of honor to share whatever one has with family and kinfolk. If the shopkeeper gives away his stock according to the code of his people he is ruined and will probably go to jail. If not he is derided as miserly and heartless. What shall he do?

A similar dilemma confronts the town-dwelling family, living on wages. By African rules of kinship both husband and wife will usually have large numbers of relatives. By the laws of hospitality all the relatives expect to be lodged, fed, and entertained whenever they choose to make a visit. They may at times descend like a plague of locusts, not only eating up the current income of the family but depleting all their savings and all they are able to borrow. Yet it would be a gross breach of propriety to suggest that their presence was causing distress. What should the family do?

Among many African peoples descent in the family has always been counted in the mother's line. It is not the father but the mother's brother who holds authority over the children and who acts as head of the family. According to old custom a boy would be sent to live with his maternal uncle for a period of training in manners and social duties. Later he would look up to his uncle for help and advice, for marriage dowry and ultimately for an inheritance. This worked well enough in the village community. But it does not work at all well in the city, where the natural unit is the elementary family—father, mother, and children. It is not the mother's gardening but the father's wages that support the family. The father carries the burden of their daily welfare. Should he not have the final word of parental authority toward his own children and relinquish his oversight of his sisters' children? But how does a society move from one of the patterns to the other without falling into confusion between them?

These are simple instances of the perplexities that confront Africans at every turning, especially the younger generation of Africans who are trying to build a coherent pattern of living out of the broken fragments they have inherited.

Disparity of Education Between Men and Women

Another source of difficulty is the fact that the education of women and girls has not kept pace with that of men and boys. African parents have been unwilling to send girls to school in any numbers. When urged to do so the stock answer has been, "What is the use? She will never be a clerk." The employed African woman is, in fact, still a rarity. Women are not found in offices, even cooks and domestic servants are usually men. On the other

107

hand girls in the villages begin at an early age to help their mothers in the many tasks of the house and garden. Where polygamy still prevails girls are claimed in marriage in their early teens, the arrangements having been made by their families long before. For these reasons schools for girls are always under pressure from the side of the traditional culture, even though young men are eager for wives trained to their own level. The following excerpt is taken from a missionary's letter dated August 6, 1957. It is not ancient history, but a present fact:

Mbuangatu Hembe, a ten-year-old girl who is remaining in the home this vacation was admitted in April. She is the daughter of an evangelistic student who asked for her to be put in the Girl's Home to keep her from being put in the harems of the king. About two weeks ago the mother came to me in great distress because the grandmother was here wanting to take Mbuangatu to the king. He had worried the old grandmother so that she was determined to deliver a girl to him if it had to be the little sister who is about seven years old. To keep the grandmother from stealing one of them I put the sister in the home too, and refused to let either of them go to the forest for water until the grandmother left. What the outcome will be remains to be seen.[1]

In this instance the church is strong enough, and sufficiently convinced of the importance of educating girls, to stand out against the pressure of tribal custom and authority. It is not always so. There are churches in Africa where the educated young men are in despair because their wives are backward and unwilling to learn, and are

[1] Letter circulated by Board of World Missions, Presbyterian Church, U. S., Nashville, Tenn. Used by permission.

bringing up their children in the grip of superstitions that they themselves have abandoned. As Jesus said: "A man's foes will be those of his own household."

Conflict of Values

A further cause of confusion is the freedom of choice that confronts the African. The traditional way of life was clear and simple. One was bound up in the group, and personal, individual choices were rarely called for. Family, clan, and tribe came first. The elders, in counsel together, made decisions, not forgetting to consider what the ancestors would wish. This pattern of group responsibility existed for many generations.

Today everyone must make many choices for himself and neither the elders nor the ancestors can help, for they never had to make such choices as these. Today's choices come at many levels. On what shall one spend his earnings? The shops are full of enticements. More important, on what shall one spend one's *life?* Is it enough to earn a living, marry and rear a family, and acquire possessions? Or is there something more vital, more challenging, to be done with one's life? Does life itself have a meaning, or was the ancient cynic right in saying: "All is vanity. What does man gain by all the toil at which he toils under the sun?"

For young people, much more than for their elders there is the question of prestige, of measuring up to commonly accepted standards of behavior. Dr. Kofi A. Busia of Ghana quotes a light-hearted West African song in which a girl expresses her fondest hopes:

> What shall I do to get a man of that type?
> One who is a "been to,"
> Car-full and fridge-full.
> What shall I do to obtain a man like that? [1]

The playful mangling of the English language lends point to the song. A "been to" is one who has "been to" far-away places, preferably overseas. "Car-full" means that he has acquired a car; "fridge-full" that he has a refrigerator. What more could a girl ask?

As citizens, West Africans are concerned with the nature of their national goals after independence. This problem is also found in other parts of the world where colonial rule is a recent memory. Independence was an obvious goal for which no sacrifice was too great. But once it is won, what then? What aim is great enough to inspire the continued, long-sustained effort needed to plant the new state firmly on its feet? Dr. Busia, writing shortly before Ghana's indepedence became a fact, commented as follows:

The Gold Coast wants to be independent so that it can sign agreements with Canada and the United States and Great Britain for working the Volta River project [electric power and aluminum refining]. In spite of the fact that you can walk through village after village and see women walking five to ten miles to fetch muddy water for use in their houses, we have accumulated about [250 million dollars] locked up in London, hoping to use some of it for the Volta River scheme. For this will be a sign of our industrialization and therefore

[1] Busia, K. A. "Africa in Transition." Unpublished lectures, Bossey, Switzerland, 1956. Used by permission.

serve as acceptable evidence of our emergence as a modern nation.

The real potentiality of Africa, however, does not lie in its mineral deposits or its forests or in the power of its rivers. The real potentiality of Africa lies in its human material. That is always an unpredictable thing. No one knows what the men and women of the present generation or the next are going to become. . . . They can learn, and what they are going to learn will be determined by what they are made to consider to be the values worth pursuing.

Advance in science and technology have made men "nuclear giants," but failures in human relations give evidence of their ethical infancy. International society must be based not only on the foundation of a common technological civilization but also on the foundation of common ethical principle. Beneath outward diversities every heart is human, and we express a common humanity in cooperation, friendship and active mutual sympathy as well as in competitions for power.[1]

This is the judgment of an African. Would that all non-Africans were equally perceptive!

Lack of Immediate Goals

One aspect of our perplexity, both in Africa and in the world at large, is the lack of certainty as to the immediate next steps. Our distant goals are fairly clear, whether we define them as fulfillment of God's purpose, and "the increase of his kingdom," or as universal peace, good will, and brotherhood. But how do we get from here to there? In *Pilgrim's Progress* the fact that Christian had his eyes fixed on the bright and shining light did not keep his feet from stumbling into the Slough of Despond. Nor would

[1] Busia, *loc. cit.*

111

Livingstone's carriers, accustomed to watching the trail a hundred yards ahead and to counting the stages of the journey by the villages they passed, have known how to navigate the unfamiliar ocean by watching the stars. We, too, stand at a point where terrestrial landmarks fail. Even Christian faith does not automatically carry with it competence in social understanding and ethical judgment, although Christian love and humility are certainly prerequisites. In Africa, where speed of change is so much a part of the picture, African ministers may with reason say —as they sometimes do: "We do not understand what is happening around us; how can we guide our people?"

Amid the complex structures and issues of the day there is clearly basic work to be done in two directions:

1. We must reach a more adequate Christian understanding of the modern world—a Christian doctrine of man in society.

2. We must work out better methods of sharing the knowledge we have, so that both ministers and laymen will be able to make sound judgments and give wise counsel.

Until these tasks are attempted the full resources of the gospel will not be released "for the healing of the nations."

COMPETING CLAIMANTS FOR AFRICA'S FAITH

In this present confusion of mind and spirit the African is confronted with many doctors, each with his own remedy. Or, to use the powerful image developed by Dr.

Floyd Shacklock in *This Revolutionary Faith,* Africa of
the mid-twentieth century has become the *arena* of con-
flicting ideologies.

Secular Ideologies

The basic issue before the African is whether he will
include religious values in his understanding of the world,
or whether he will think in purely secular terms. It would
never occur to him *not* to include religion if the powerful
example of the West were not before him. But the West
has for the most part relegated religion to secondary
status. It has been excluded from most serious thinking
about "practical affairs." Science, which started as the
study of the material world, leaving the realm of values
out of account, has become for many people a most important value in its own right. Specialization in almost
every field has been carried so far that wholeness has been
lost. Even the ministers of religion implicitly accept this
broken world and seldom claim for God the lordship over
the whole creation that belongs to him as creator. And
they are sometimes less interested in people than in ideas,
or programs, or theological systems, or tangible achievements.

The African usually meets secularism in the form of
Western civilization stripped of its thin veneer of conven-
tional Christianity. Superficially it has great appeal. The
African is as ready as anyone else to accept its material
benefits. But as a way of life, a system of values, he does
not find it satisfying for very long. It is too shallow, too
empty, too meaningless. Worse yet, it has shown itself in-

capable of saving man from the worst vices of his own nature. Dr. Busia provides an illustration of this fact:

In 1817 the first British resident arrived in Kumasi. He witnessed many things with a very keen eye. His book . . . described at length a tribal purification ceremony. The chief came out bedecked in all his glory and his people followed him to the river where he sprinkled water on them as a sign of the beginning of another year and thanks to the gods. . . . Leading the dancing procession there were two people who had been condemned to die. They had knives pierced through their cheeks and were being paraded . . . to their execution. The author with the sensitivity of a civilized man concluded his description with the judgment: "I was glad that I belonged to a civilized country." In the year 1945 an Ashanti, namely myself, was browsing round a bookshop in Oxford. I picked up a book of photographs . . . of some of the concentration camps of Europe. I saw photographs of caves where human bones were piled up and where human bodies were reduced to ashes. . . . I cut out one of these pages and pasted it in my book of descriptions of the Gold Coast in 1817. Opposite the very big picture of a barbarian chief in all his glory I put one of these photos from a European concentration camp. Beneath the one I wrote "Ashanti 1817," and beneath the other "Europe 1945," with no other comment.[1]

Another secular world view that some Africans meet is embodied practically in the trade union movement, and theoretically in socialism. Africans have no hesitation in joining unions when there is need, and where they are permitted to do so. Thus far unions have been more often used against the African than for him since the unions are frequently segregated and specifically interested in pre-

[1] Busia, *loc. cit.*

114

serving European working rights. In South Africa, Africans cannot legally belong to a European union.

It is probably safe to say that most Africans recognize unions for what they are—a means of obtaining power in the economic struggle. To the extent that the African is forced to struggle for equality of rights against opposition organized along lines of class and color, he, too, will organize. He will do it with innate skill and grim determination. Furthermore the weapons of industrial strife can be turned to political ends. Some of the ablest young Africans first became known as labor leaders and have international contacts in the labor movement.

Communism has thus far had little numerical influence in Africa. Few Africans even know the meaning of the word. But the technique of world communism is to seize upon every real grievance, foment discord, and prevent reconciliation. Grievances are not hard to find. Sometimes clever agitators have managed to build little disturbances into big ones. They have even incited people to violence at times. This happened, for instance, in Cameroun in 1955-57. It can be noted that France has seemed to be more tolerant of Communist agitation in its African territories than any other ruling power.

However, class struggle as a permanent pattern of life has little appeal except in cases where long continued injustice has resulted in bitterness of spirit. The African simply does not believe in it and doesn't want it. Moreover, he seldom stays angry very long unless under extreme provocation. He hungers not for divisions but for togetherness. Furthermore the atheism of Communist teaching runs counter to his own spiritual perceptions.

Considering the tensions that exist in Africa, communism has made less progress there than might have been expected. If communism should gain real strength anywhere in Africa it is most apt to be in the Union of South Africa. This will be due less to its own appeal than to the folly of governmental policies such as the Suppression of Communism Act that places under ban, along with actual Communists, "any doctrine or scheme . . . which aims at bringing about any political, industrial, social or economic change by the promotion of disturbance or disorder . . . or . . . which aims at the encouragement of feelings of hostility between the European and non-European races of the Union." [1] However, under the terms of this law few people have actually been convicted.

South Africa is, in fact, the original home of non-violent resistance, for it was because of conditions he found there that Mohandas K. Gandhi first conceived the idea that was afterwards so effective in India. Later an American Negro, the Rev. Dr. Martin Luther King, was influenced by Gandhi's philosophy and successfully used the same method in the Montgomery, Alabama, bus strike. The Montgomery strike in turn gave the impetus to similar action in Africa. This method is the very antithesis of communism, for it is the social weapon of a profoundly religious people, sustained by faith in the justice of their cause.

Africans have used passive resistance with skill and

[1] Union of South Africa. *Suppression of Communism Act*, No. 44, 1950, p. 1.

self-discipline. Late in 1957 more than 100,000 people engaged in a bus boycott to protest a rise in fares in the Johannesburg area though for many of them it involved walking as much as twelve miles to and from their work. They won a favorable settlement against great odds. More recently boycotts of Afrikaner owned businesses have begun to shake the confidence of some of the supporters of apartheid.

An interesting example of passive resistance concerns the burdensome regulations that require all Africans in the Union of South Africa to carry identity cards. Formerly only men had to show such passes on demand. New rules require women to have them also. A group of twenty-five women of the Baphurutse tribe of northwestern Transvaal burned their passes in protest. Word reached the commissioner, who sent an Afrikaner sergeant to arrest the offenders. After a journey of forty miles into the hills the sergeant found 233 women gathered together. "The twenty-five are among us," they said. "Take us all." So the sergeant sent for two busses and took them all. Meanwhile word reached a well known woman lawyer who demanded prompt action against the guilty ones and release of the others. The judge, unable to sort them out, postponed the case three weeks. The women demanded busses to take them home, and sat still until they were provided. Three weeks later their number had grown to nearly four hundred, and when the sergeant came for them they began to "remember" stragglers here and there whom he would have to bring in before they could move. Finally they agreed that it was time to go, and set off on foot, singing songs of derision aimed at the unhappy sergeant. Then as evening approached they turned off the road and sat down, while their men came around asking who would cook their suppers and put the children to bed. At last the sergeant gave up and went home defeated. Despite this gaily heroic resistance the government finally won and the original twenty-five were convicted and sent to jail.

Religious Faiths

Yet, important as passive resistance may prove to be as a weapon against oppression in the hands of a people without political power, it still is only a weapon. It does not provide any guidance for the conduct of life, nor any clue as to life's meaning. Only religious faith can do that. So the African, like the rest of us, remains hungry, incomplete, and unfulfilled until his soul finds rest in God. It is generally clear to him, as it should be to us all, that faith involves deeper issues than any secular ideology can resolve. Such ideologies deal with political, economic, or social patterns, useful in their place, but not fundamental. They are concerned with the *how* of life, not with the *what* or the *why*. Therefore the African seeks in religious faith an answer to the deeper questions. Broadly speaking there are four claimants to his religious loyalty—animism, Islam, Roman Catholicism, and Protestantism. What do they offer?

ANIMISM. Despite occasional attempts to ally traditional African religious beliefs with political nationalism,

118

animism as an exclusive faith has little to offer. The world of the animist is peopled with nature spirits, but they are tied to particular places and the people who live there. Local gods cannot meet the needs of people moving about as Africans move today. Animism is enshrined in ceremonies that differ from tribe to tribe and language to language. It admits the existence of a greater god, creator of the world, but knows nothing about him and affords no access to him. It has little or nothing to say about the meaning of life or the nature of man. It offers no redemption and no hope.

On the other hand animism affirms the reality of the spiritual realm, and maintains a link between those now living on earth and those who have died. African Christians demand of the church an affirmation of "the communion of saints" vigorous enough to confirm what they already believe—that those who have died are still interested in their descendants, and that reverence for the dead is not an empty gesture but real spiritual communion. While Africans seek a more universal faith than animism can provide, there is no doubt that animistic ideas and practices will continue to exert an influence for many generations, just as they have within other religions, including Christianity. One of the basic tasks of African churches is to draw the right line of distinction between elements that are consistent with Christianity and those that are not. A long continued process of learning and testing will be necessary, and it is quite possible that future generations will reach conclusions different from those held today. We may well recall that Jesus said to the first disciples: "I have many things to tell you, but you cannot bear them now."

ISLAM. Throughout a broad belt across Africa below the Sahara Desert, and extending far southward along the east coast, Islam is an active contender for the soul of Africa. The appeal of Islam lies partly in the fact that it admits its members to the great international "brotherhood of the faithful" without making moral or ethical demands upon them. As practiced in Africa, Islam is quite simple. It rests on five pillars: repetition of the creed, prayer, fasting, almsgiving, and—for those who are able —pilgrimage to Mecca. All these are visible acts performed in public, and in them Islam dramatizes itself before the onlooker. In the Koran the inner meaning of these acts is stressed, but few Africans know much Arabic and they are told that the language of the Koran is too holy for translation. For many the unknown words take on an aura of magic that adds to their appeal but gives no clue to the riches of Islamic thought.

Itinerant traders are largely responsible for the spread of Islam. Being Africans themselves, they present it as a universal faith that truly belongs to Africa. Petty chiefs often see in it a means of strengthening their own prestige, since Islam is an inclusive way of life that makes no distinction between political and religious loyalties. Conversion of the chief to Islam is apt to entail acceptance of the new faith by all his people. Islam supports the traditional dominance of men over women. It permits polygamy, up to four wives at a time, and does nothing to raise the status of women. It cloaks African animism and tribalism with the dignity of a universal religion having an age-old tradition. Thereby it enshrines the past and makes adjustment to present and future change much more difficult.

This is evident in Muslim disinterest in education. Inside the walled Muslim city of Kano, in northern Nigeria, lives a population of about 120,000. Outside the walls a new city of some 40,000 non-Muslims has grown up. The latter are largely migrants from southern Nigeria, many of whom are Christian. And among them there are roughly ten times as many children attending school as there are among the much larger Muslim population in the old city.

Its resistance to change will, in the long run, work against Islam in Africa as it is already doing in parts of Asia. Educated women will not accept the inferior status assigned to them by Islamic tradition. In the old days many wives meant wealth, security, and prestige. To the new and growing class of wage-earners more than one wife means added burdens of expense, divided loyalties, and discontent. In the long view polygamy itself is on the defensive. Already in Asia Muslim apologists are trying to show that Islam favors monogamy. This idea has not yet entered Africa, but Muslim tolerance of polygamy and indifference to the family bring it under increasing criticism.

Islam also comes under fire on political grounds. The somewhat feudal structure of African society, the old pattern of big and little chiefs, is giving way to modern administrative systems based on European practice. In a modern state religious faith is one thing, civil obedience is quite another. In Islam, however, they are bound together. Thus as African society is westernized, Islam becomes irrelevant and even stands in the way of freedom.

Furthermore the vaunted brotherhood of Islam has limits. Tribal memories are long, and Africans do not forget that for many generations Islamic Arabs raided central Africa for cattle and slaves. Even today there are reports that pilgrims to Mecca sometimes fail to return home because they have been trapped into slavery. Government efforts to protect the pilgrims have not yet succeeded in wiping out this evil traffic.

Despite these weaknesses, Islam is a great force in Africa, and must be taken seriously. Christian churches and missions have given it too little attention in the past, although the All-Africa Church Conference at Ibadan, Nigeria, in January 1958, reflected an increased concern. Plans were initiated for a more thorough study of Islam in Africa, special training for missionaries and Africans called to Christian witness among Muslims, and a search for better understanding of how the gospel may best be presented to Muslims.

ROMAN CATHOLICISM. More than five hundred years ago, long before the Protestant Reformation brought to light the deep cleavages within the church, Christian missionaries were already making contact with Africans as Portuguese explorers advanced farther and farther along the coast. At no time since then has the Roman Catholic Church been unrepresented in Africa, though there have been long periods of stagnation when little effort was made to win Africans to the faith. Today the church is very active. It is making a determined effort to become the dominant religious force in Africa, and it is achieving a large measure of success. Numerically Roman Catholicism is stronger than Protestantism in continental Africa. (There are about 18,193,000 and 12,625,000 adherents respectively, though allowance must be made for the less inclusive basis on which Protestant statistics are usually compiled.) [1] Many thousands of Roman Catholic missionaries are at work, with added thousands of African priests, nuns, and lay brothers and not a few African bishops. Every town of any size has at least one Catholic church, usually large, well placed, and impressive. Roman Catholics as well as Protestants have provided schools, social centers, hospitals, dispensaries and clinics in great numbers, and the service given by these institutions is of incalculable value. Among their missionaries are scholars whose researches have contributed greatly to our knowledge of African peoples and to wise social and political development. They also include many humble and saintly men and women whose devoted service to the poor, the ignorant, the sick, and the needy is beyond praise.

All of this contributes to the prestige that the Roman Catholic Church enjoys throughout the continent. The African is impressed by its universal presence and power. Wherever he goes, the Catholic church is there, and everyone is welcomed. Race or color makes no difference;

[1] Figures from *World Christian Handbook*. London: World Dominion Press, 1957, p. 170. Protestant figures do not include those of Orthodox or Eastern rite churches.

language is no barrier. The duties of the Christian do not change. The same rites are celebrated, and the same practices of piety are encouraged. To the African who feels insecure because everything else is changing the enduring sameness of the Roman Catholic Church has great attractiveness. This is reinforced by the color and drama of its liturgy, the use of vestments, incense, symbolism, and pageantry, and the sense of mystery and power that pervades its worship. All these elements give the Catholic church a powerful hold on its members and afford a strong appeal to non-Christians.

But in other respects Catholicism is less acceptable. It is obviously and obstinately foreign to Africa; its authority and its tradition both stem from Europe. Submission to the authority of the church is the cardinal duty of the layman; control remains in the hands of the priests and behind them stands the hierarchy centering in Rome. Catholic doctrine is rigid. It makes no concessions to African experience or ideas. It does not welcome free inquiry nor encourage independent, creative thinking. It fears "that most pernicious doctrine which would make the laity the factor of progress in the Church." [1] The monolithic authority of the church induces not only respect but fear, and fear breeds rebellion. Too often a feeling takes root that the church is more concerned for its own power and prestige than for the interests of its members; and Africans, like other people, resent being used for the self-aggrandizement of others.

[1] Pius X. Encyclical, "Pascendi." English text published by Catholic Truth Society, London, 1937, p. 35.

Yet in the practices of Roman Catholicism Africans find many parallels to animism. The following passage describes a lecture given by an educated West African animist:

He examines religious practices in the Roman Catholic Church: masses for the dead, adoration of statues, confession of sins. He compares the mass for the dead with ancestor worship in animistic cults, in which the chief of the clan offers a libation to the spirit of his ancestor, invoking his blessing upon his descendants. The ceremony, he says, in no way differs from the requiem mass conducted by a priest. An analogy is drawn between the behavior of an animist before the objects representing his dead relatives and the genuflexions made by Catholics before a statue or a picture of a saint, or at the foot of a crucifix erected at the entrance to towns and villages.

The lecturer continues by saying that African religion shows itself superior to Christianity [Catholicism] in relation to the confession of sins. In Christianity confession is made secretly by the believer to his priest, who absolves him. He leaves satisfied. Next day he takes part in Holy Communion without having made any reparation to the person sinned against, and there is nothing to prevent his committing the same offence again. In animism, in which suffering is [regarded as] a consequence of a sin against a human being or a spirit, confession is always in public and this preserves the sinner from backsliding.[1]

Since Roman Catholicism enshrines so many practices and ideas drawn originally from the animistic and pagan cults it has met in the course of the centuries, it makes

[1] Danho, Josue. "Encounter Between Christian and non-Christian," a preparatory paper for the International Missionary Council Assembly, Ghana, December 1957. Used by permission.

little demand on African converts. The threshold of admission is low. Pagans readily accept baptism into the church because little change of belief or conduct is expected of them. New members often receive little instruction in the faith. The church is patient; it is willing to wait for the next generation to grow up in the hope that, being born and instructed in the faith, they will have a knowledge of Christian truth that their fathers and mothers could not attain. As a result the Roman Catholic Church is burdened with great numbers of nominal Christians who have neither understanding of Christianity nor any real conviction, and who are easily drawn back into paganism. Their example hardly commends Christianity to others. It tends instead to conceal the real power of the gospel from those who are seeking after truth.

PROTESTANTISM. More than any other religion Protestant Christianity demands and expects its adherents to be a different kind of men and women because they are Christians. Conversion is not a matter of a verbal "acceptance of Christ." It is literally a "turning the other way" in which self-will gives place to self-commitment to the will of God. This is our response to the love of God that is made manifest in Jesus Christ. Commitment is symbolized by baptism whereby the convert is received into the fellowship of the church. The church is in essence the community of the obedient "children of God." It is the "Body of Christ" not only as a mystical ideal but in the concrete practical sense that the church exists to work the works of God, a task in which every member has a part.

The Lord Jesus Christ calls men and women to His service; He offers them free and full salvation—not for their own satisfaction, not for their own worth or peace of mind but because He has a job for them to do in His service. The invitation to *come* to Him is always followed by His command to *go* into all the world at His behest.[1]

Because it is a response of the whole person to an inner compulsion, essential Christianity, as understood in Protestant churches, cannot be reduced to mere conformity to outward patterns of behavior, acquiescence in a creed, or enjoyment of the fellowship of the church. These are all secondary, not central.

Jesus came to save us from ourselves, but sometimes we allow ourselves to be more subtly selfish after we have become Christians than we were before. We are so grateful for what Christ has done for us and in us that we are in mortal peril of sitting down to enjoy the pleasures of the Christian life for ourselves and by ourselves. This is *not* salvation. This is *not* conversion. The truly converted man will be converted in every department of life, trying in every one of his activities and relationships to bring honor to Christ's name.[2]

Neither in Africa nor anywhere else do all Christians measure up to this standard. The temptation to be content with a nominal and relatively undemanding standard of discipleship is always present. The African church has special problems to meet; tough and intractible problems in the matter of cultural adjustment, uprooted people, racial tensions, new tasks of citizenship, and many

[1] de Blank, Joost. *This is Conversion.* London: Hodder and Stoughton Ltd., 1957, p. 73. Used by permission.
[2] *Ibid.*, pp. 73-74.

others. It has no ready-made answers to these problems. Many of its members are uneducated, many of its leaders poorly trained. It is beset by divisions and temptations. Humanly speaking it has little to boast of.

Yet the church continues to live and to grow. Its witness may be poor and inadequate, but the word of God continues to be spoken and heard. The very fact that the Scriptures are read and expounded week by week in hundreds of languages and in tens of thousands of gatherings enables great numbers to learn something of the gospel. The Word strikes home because it rings true. It answers the deepest need of lost, hungry, bewildered souls. It makes sense of our otherwise meaningless existence. It gives us a standing-ground outside ourselves in the grace and love of God, a basis of moral judgment in the mind of Christ, a release from sin in the Cross.

The True Way of Africa

All this was beautifully stated by the Rev. S. E. Gengu of Zululand, in his address, "Quo Vadis Africa?" at the All-Africa Lutheran Conference in Marangu, Tanganyika, in 1955:

There are many glittering things facing our beloved Africa today, such as communism, materialism, nationalism, old religions that seem to be reviving, and many others as well. All these things come quickly and soon vanish again, like a cloud in the sky. All these people that make such promises soon die, and all their good promises come to an end. But Christ is here yesterday, today and tomorrow. His Word and Church will remain forever. This then is the great hope of Africa. It is the true way of Africa.

128

Which Way, Young Africa?

Africa is in a turmoil. At the cross-road there are many road-signs. It is like in places where there are many pleasure resorts—each sign tells something nice about the place, making you want to go there. All these roads are enticing Africa, promising something attractive. But what is it? Can it save the soul of Africa? The sign that God has placed on the road that will take Africa to a glorious goal, is the Cross—the Cross of Christ and His redemption. That is Africa's only hope, as it is the only hope of any continent, race, tribe or individual.[1]

[1] Marangu, a Record of the All-Africa Lutheran Conference, 1955, p. 152. Used by permission of the Lutheran World Federation.

CHAPTER SIX

The Responsive Church

IN JANUARY 1958, AT IBADAN, NIGERIA, THE FIRST ALL-Africa Church Conference took place. One hundred and ninety-five people came together for ten days of worship, study, discussion, fellowship, and "conversation about the things of God." No such representative group had ever before met in Africa for any purpose; such a gathering would have been quite impossible without the present network of airlines covering the continent. Ninety-six of the delegates represented the churches of twenty-five countries of Africa (six were white South Africans, the rest Negroes). Of these delegates sixteen were women. Forty-eight missionaries attended, and the remaining fifty-one included staff, consultants, visitors, and fraternal delegates from Asia, Latin America, and the Pacific. English, French, and Portuguese were the official languages (with simultaneous translation when necessary) and several African languages were spoken in deeply moving services of worship.

The delegates lived together in Spartan simplicity in quarters made available by two secondary schools. Meals were served in cafeteria style out-of-doors, and often eaten under the trees. In a very African gesture of hospitality, church congregations throughout Nigeria adopted individual delegates by name as their guests, and sent money to pay the cost of entertainment. In this way food was provided for all the members of the conference without charge to themselves.

Each day opened and closed with worship. Each morning's work session began with an hour of Bible study, followed by two long conference periods. Five major topics were dealt with: the Church, Youth and the Family; the Church and Economic Life; the Church and Citizenship; the Church, Culture, and Religion; and the Growing Church. Each topic was first presented in basic addresses, largely by African speakers, and then discussed thoroughly in small groups. Findings and proposals for action were reported back from the groups to the conference, where they were considered and recommended to the churches. The addresses and group findings appear in the printed report: *The Church in Changing Africa*.[1]

The real value, however, lay not in what the conference said or did, but in the "astonished joy" with

[1] *The Church in Changing Africa*. Report of the All-Africa Church Conference held at Ibadan, Nigeria, Jan. 10-19, 1958. New York: International Missionary Council. 1958.

which the delegates discovered each other and found that everywhere they were experiencing the same renewal of life and the same call to witness and service. This note runs through the *Message to the Churches of Africa,* adopted in the closing moments of the Conference and sent out to be translated and read in churches all over Africa on Easter Sunday, 1958. It reads in part:

We . . . rejoice that God has called us together and in His name we send greetings . . . to all the churches in Africa. . . . We come from [many] countries. . . . But although our languages are many, our reason for coming here is the same, that we love the Lord Jesus Christ and are witnesses to His Gospel; that in Him we are one people. . . . We are one in Him who was born a Jew in Bethlehem, fled from Herod into Egypt, grew up at Nazareth, died in Jerusalem, arose there and lives today in Ibadan and in every other city and village in the world that His Father created. Of this oneness in Christ we have been given such a rich experience at this Conference that not one of us is likely to forget it.

To be here is to have abundant cause to thank God for the way that the Gospel has been brought to so many countries, and to be filled with astonished joy that it has transformed the lives of so many men and women in Africa.

In a continent where such massive events lie ahead, we thank God that the Christian Church has taken such deep root. We know there are millions who have not heard the Gospel and we accept the challenge of the evangelizing of our countries, especially in the face of the dangers of materialism and secularism.

While this experience of unity has been rich and deep, we acknowledge with penitence our many divisions which have prevented us from witnessing to our unity in Him, but this we still purpose to do with His assistance. We believe that Christ challenges us to overcome these divisions in the Church and to work for the removal of all injustices based on racial discrimination which we believe to be contrary to the will of God.

We rejoice in the advance of Christian countries toward self-government and in the liberation of African energies and talents, praying that they may be used for the service of Him whom we acknowledge to be the Lord of all mankind.

The continent of Africa will see unparalleled events and changes during the rest of this century, welcomed by some, feared by others. We pray that the Christian Church of Africa will play its role as champion, teacher, counsellor and shepherd during these crucial years. We are humbly aware of our responsibilities to God and to this continent, and dedicate ourselves anew to their performance, trusting that we shall be led and supported by our fellow-Christians throughout Africa and the world.

In the name of the Father of all men, in the name of the Son who saved us all, in the name of the Holy Spirit who inspires us, we declare ourselves to be one in Christ. Amen.[1]

In a sense this conference marks a culminating point in the long story of the Christian mission in Africa. Here, more clearly than ever before, is heard the voice of the church in Africa making its own declaration of joyous commitment and obedience. It expresses the true note of discipleship—hearing the call of God and responding: "Here am I, send me."

During the year of preparation that preceded the conference the group involved in planning (of whom the writer was one) came to feel that the watchword of the meeting should be: "He who has an ear, let him hear

[1] Quoted from: "Message to the Churches of Africa," in *The Church in Changing Africa,* op. cit., pp. 15-16.

what the Spirit says to the churches." These words, addressed to the seven churches of Asia in the Book of Revelation, were the text of the closing sermon and manifestly represented the prevailing spirit of this African conference.

But the words have an even wider reference. Does the work that God has done and is doing in Africa have something to say to all of us? Amid the confusions, the bewilderment, the "brokenness" in which we are all involved may we also "hear what the Spirit says to the churches" and so be brought to a fresh knowledge of "the Way"? Has the experience gained in the Christian mission in Africa something to teach us that is important not only to Africa but to the whole church? If so, what is it?

Dr. Walter Freytag, the great German student of the Christian mission, has pointed out that when we speak of "the mission" we naturally think in terms of the missionary movement of modern times, forgetting that this is only one segment of the whole task of the church through the ages. In the sight of God the mission is vastly greater and perhaps quite different from our conception of it. So too, when we refer to "the church" we think of the existing churches as we know them, though they are certainly not all that the New Testament teaching about the church implies, nor all that God intends his church to be. So by looking at what God has done in Africa we may try to see, first, what it tells us about the real nature of the church, and second, what we can learn about the present-day mission to which the church is called.

THE NATURE OF THE CHURCH

Some things that we are apt either to take for granted or to forget entirely come sharply into focus when we see the church in its African setting, for there it often still has the vigorous freshness of youth. It is less conformed to the paganism of society everywhere around it. The transforming power of the life within it is more evident.

God's Field, God's Building

From the spread of Christianity in Africa it is clear that the church is not something we have made; it is not a human institution; it is God's creation. The raw material is human lives yielded to his will, but the use to which he puts them goes far beyond our thoughts and plans. More than thirty years ago Pierre Dinzau, a young ministerial student in Congo, preached a memorable sermon. He told the parable of the fig-tree that the owner wanted to cut down because it failed to bear fruit. But the gardener asked for one more year, to see if with extra care it would begin to bear. (Luke 13:6-9) "Now you are trees," said the preacher. "You are going to be planted in the villages. Your job is to bear fruit. The Master will be watching. Don't waste your time doing nothing. Speak the word. Witness. Work. Bear fruit!"

Among the hearers that day was another student, Ngumina, one of the first to make the long river journey from the inland station of Vanga. Two years after his graduation Ngumina reported back:

The church in the Vanga area has grown so big that it is no longer possible to bring all the people to the mission station for meetings. It is being divided into districts. I have been made pastor-in-charge of one half of the work. In my field there are more than a hundred villages with catechists and groups of Christians. More than fourteen hundred enquirers are in training for admission to the church, and I know every one of them personally.

Service like that lends meaning to Paul's words: ". . . we are fellow workmen for God; you are God's field, God's building." In the years since then the work centering in Vanga has further multiplied until it is one of the strongest groups of churches in Africa, with over 28,000 church members, 22,000 children in Christian schools and a staff of pastors, teachers, and catechists numbering over six hundred persons. "I planted," says Paul, "Apollos watered, but God gave the increase."

Not a Goal But a Way; Not a Structure But a Movement

When we speak of a church we are apt to think of a building or an organization. Not so the African. "Church" in his languages means the congregation, the worshipping, witnessing fellowship, which is the building in which God lives by his spirit. (Ephesians 1:22, Phillips' translation.) [1] The physical building is *nzo a Nzambi*,[2] the house of God. In this the African is true to the New Testament, where "church" always refers to people, the

[1] See footnote, p. 139.
[2] Kikongo language.

people called of God and responding to His call—a people in movement, on the way. In fact, to judge by the Book of Acts, before Christians had any other name, before they were even called Christians they were known as the people "belonging to the Way." (See Acts 9:2.) One wonders whether the term had a secret, symbolic meaning; whether perhaps it was a password in times of persecution. "Belonging to the Way" could so easily be used in place of "belonging to Christ" who is Himself the Way.

In any case "belonging to the Way" fitly describes the church in Africa. It is full of life and movement, it does not feel that it has arrived. Congo children, when called, are taught to reply promptly: *"Ndweki"*—"I have come," even though they are only ready to start. So also the church. It is responding to the call of God, it is on the way. The Ibadan conference message is full of statements of intention: "We accept the challenge of evangelizing our countries." "Christ challenges us . . . to work for the removal of all injustices based on racial discrimination." "We are humbly aware of our responsibilities . . . and dedicate ourselves anew to their performance." These are the utterances of a church that feels itself to be much more a *movement* than an *institution*.

In this emphasis the African church recovers an authentic note of the New Testament. Every time men and women obey a fresh impulsion of the spirit a movement is born. With good reason we speak of "the modern missionary *movement*," recognizing its kinship with the Pauline mission in the New Testament when the Spirit sent forth Paul and Barnabas on a great new venture. But every movement has to develop a *structure*, an organization, a pattern of work with rules and policies and officers and administrative machinery. This is the body in which the movement clothes itself. The body is necessary, but it inevitably limits the freedom of the movement. As the structure grows and hardens the movement tends to become more and more confined within it. Spontaneity is lost, imagination is dulled, and the movement gradually becomes an institution.

Looking back we can see that in the centuries from the coming of Jesus Christ to the Reformation the institutional aspect of the church had grown to the point where it completely overshadowed the movement aspect. The "new wine" of the Reformation—a fresh movement under the impulsion of the Holy Spirit—could not be contained in the old hardened institutional wineskins of the Roman Catholic Church. As a result new church bodies came into being. But the institutional conception of the church was so strong, even in the minds of the Reformers, that the new churches followed the old in placing great emphasis on order and structure. Much stress was laid on creeds and confessions, systems of church government, forms of worship, and codes of behavior. By and large it is disagreement in these realms that has kept the churches apart. If with the help of the young churches of Africa and Asia, we can recover the power to see the church primarily as *the Christian movement* many of these barriers will be found less important than they have seemed.

This emphasis on movement, on the church as the people "belonging to the Way" does not mean that the church has no goal. But the goal is not the building of an institution—a natural goal from a human standpoint. The true goal of the church is to manifest the glory of God and to serve his loving purpose in the life of the world. As Paul puts it:

God has allowed us to know the secret of his plan, and it is this: He purposes in his sovereign will that all human history shall be consummated in Christ, that everything that exists in heaven or earth shall find its perfection and fulfilment in him. . . . (Eph. 1:9-10, Phillips' Translation).[1]

Because this goal lies beyond all human contriving Christians who keep it in view are saved from any complacent sense of having arrived. We cannot reach the ultimate, but it gives us a sense of direction. The Christian is able to judge every situation by considering whether it tends toward or away from "the perfection and fulfilment of all things in Christ."

One Body in Christ

One element of its life that the church in Africa is testing by this standard is the the dividedness it has inherited from its parent bodies, a dividedness made much worse by the emergence of many new African churches and sects. Scores of these new groups exist in many parts of Africa. In South Africa they number over a thousand. Many of these churches center around the person of an

[1] Phillips, J. B. *Letters to Young Churches.* N. Y.: The Macmillan Co., 1948. Used by permission.

individual leader or "prophet." Basically they are a revolt against external authority, and an expression of the natural yearning for self-expression and spontaneous response. Some of them appear to be more African than Christian in emphasis.

The existence and growth of separatist sects is a matter of deep concern to many churches that share a common historic Christian tradition. They are a standing reproach to a Protestantism that by its internal divisions contradicts the gospel of reconciliation and hinders the mission and renewal of the Church.

Yet beneath all these divisions there is a growing awareness that *as a movement* the church in Africa is one, even though organizationally it is not one body but many at various stages of growth. The discovery of the depth of this real unity was one of the sources of the joy and strength expressed in the Ibadan message. As one of the Uganda delegates put it:

In our country we are all Anglicans, and we thought that "Anglicans" and "Christians" were just the same thing. We knew there were some folk called Moravians down by Lake Victoria, and we admitted they were God-fearing people, but it would not have occurred to us to call them Christians. Now we know that we are all one in Christ in a way we never thought possible before.

On this matter the judgment of the conference was clear:

While this experience of unity has been rich and deep, we acknowledge with penitence our many divisions which have prevented us from witnessing to our unity in Him, but this we still purpose to do with His assistance. We believe that Christ challenges us to overcome these divisions in the Church . . .

There is every indication that as the churches in Africa reach full self-government they will move resolutely in the direction of corporate unity. In West Africa conversations on unity have been going forward somewhat slowly for years. Recently the Moderator of the Church of South India spent some time in Nigeria. His visit clarified many issues and answered many questions. The hour of decision in West Africa may not be too far off.

In Belgian Congo, the various missions agreed in 1934 that there should be only one Protestant church body in Congo, the Church of Christ in Congo. Similar national churches exist in Angola and Mozambique. The membership card of the Church of Christ in Congo is recognised throughout the country and members moving from one area to another are freely accepted. But little has been done to give substantial form to this theoretically united church. It has no central organization at all. Instead the various segments of the church have taken on the denominational patterns of the missions to which they are related, Presbyterian synods, Methodist conferences, Baptist associations, and so forth. Thus the original hope of a growing, visible unity has been largely dissipated.

But in 1957 Africans sat for the first time as full members of the Congo Protestant Council. Immediately they proposed the formation of a central commission on the church, and in 1958—a month after the Ibadan conference—the commission was established. One of the Ibadan delegates, Jean Lubikulu, who was also a member of the council, made a challenging statement on the need for wider fellowship. He said in substance:

We have been too much separated from each other. We have lived to ourselves in isolation, and we have not known how much we were missing. But at Ibadan we found ourselves one in Christ with people from all over Africa and beyond. In the dormitory with me was a man from Egypt. When I met him I thought how Joseph and Mary took the child Jesus and fled into Egypt—the country this man came from. Now there is a church there. He is a missionary from that church serving in the Sudan. In the next room was a man from Ethiopia, and I thought how Philip met a man from Ethiopia on the road and baptized him. The Church of Christ is in all these places. It strengthens our faith to know this. We need to know each other. We need to become in fact one fellowship, one body in Christ.

But without waiting for organic reunion of church bodies, the Christian *movement* has already begun to develop organs of action beyond the structure of the separate churches. Under the prompting of the Holy Spirit the people of God have been moved to band themselves together in a great variety of voluntary agencies for the doing of God's work. Most Christian welfare agencies began that way. So did the missionary societies, and many of these societies (especially in Europe) are still independent of denominational structures. Christian councils, of which there are nearly twenty in the countries of Africa alone, the National Council of the Churches of Christ in the United States of America, the

International Missionary Council, and the World Council of Churches are among the organs by which the churches are enabled to work as a *body* and not merely as a *group*. Paul's image of the "Body of Christ" implies such linking together of the parts:

. . . speaking the truth in love, we are to grow up in every way into him who is the head, into Christ, from whom the whole body, joined and knit together by every joint with which it is supplied, when each part is working properly, makes bodily growth and upbuilds itself in love. (Eph. 4:15-16)

A Band of Disciples Being Taught by the Spirit

African Christians are people of the Way in still another sense; they are still learning the meaning of discipleship. Here too they reflect the New Testament, for the Christian is not a finished product, he is always in process of becoming. "Not that I am already perfect," said Paul, "but I press on." We assume all too easily that Christianity implies one definite, fixed code of morals, always and everywhere the same, and that the conscience sensitized by the Holy Spirit will always make the same response. This is not wholly true. There are many stages on the road of discipleship, it is only step by step that God's will becomes known to us. Jesus said: "I have yet many things to say to you, but you cannot bear them now."

Paul thought it necessary to admonish "the saints at Ephesus" not to lie or steal—vices we do not expect to find among the saints! He spends a good deal of effort over the question of eating meat that had been offered to idols. That was a real problem to his hearers, a problem of Christians coming out of the pagan cultures of Greece and Rome. The churches in Ghana face a similiar question today in regard to the ceremony of libation—pouring wine on the ground in honor of the ancestors. Formerly this was a family rite, now the state has adopted the custom as a patriotic symbol. Should Christians observe the rite, or abstain, or actively oppose it? To such questions there is no quick and easy answer. A clear conviction emerges only gradually as experience grows.

This is equally true in weightier matters. Slavery was accepted by Christians as part of the fabric of society for many generations. Only in the eighteenth and nineteenth centuries did it gradually become intolerable to the Christian conscience. Even more recently have the moral issues involved in imperialism and colonialism been recognized. Chapter Three of this book questions Christian toleration of the system of migratory labor, which, as practiced in Africa, brings great evils in its wake. Stage by stage the meaning of discipleship becomes clearer.

Mabel Shaw, who was for many years principal of a girls' school in Northern Rhodesia, understood this process. One day a group of girls came to tell her about certain practices, common in the villages, which they had been carrying on secretly in the dormitories. They had reached a conviction that these were wrong, and had decided to stop. To their surprise Mabel Shaw replied: "I have known for a long time that this was going on. I

could have told you to stop, but it would not have done
much good for you merely to accept my judgment. Now
you have decided for yourselves; that is a spiritual victory."

John Taylor, whose description of village life in
Uganda has been quoted in Chapter Two, has made a
careful study of the way in which the meaning of discipleship grows as the gospel takes root.[1] He notes four
stages. The first he calls *congruence,* the *fitting together*
of the new teaching and the old culture. To be accepted
at all the gospel has to come as a fulfilment, a deeper
meaning, a lighting up, of what was already there. Just as
Paul quoted a Greek poet in presenting the gospel to the
Athenians, so an African evangelist draws on the prov-
erbs and beliefs of his people. Everywhere there are
elements of human experience that may become a preparation for the gospel.

Taylor's second stage is *detachment,* the gradual
loosening of bondage to the old ways as the gospel leads
to independent judgment and personal choice. This is apt
to be almost imperceptible, "like a man shifting his
weight from one foot to the other."

The third stage is *demand,* as the growing Christian
discovers that obedience to the gospel brings under the
judgment of Christ one aspect of life after another. This
is the step-by-step growth in discipleship mentioned
above. Often in Africa the first major demand of the
gospel has involved the abandonment of charms and

[1] Taylor, John V. *Processes of Growth in an African Church.* London: SCM Press, 1958, pp. 8-10. Used by permission.

145

fetishes. (Compare Acts 19:17-20.) Other demands follow. In Uganda aristocrats felt called to share in menial tasks. Elsewhere tribal feuds were ended, household slaves freed, powerful secret brotherhoods brought under control, ancient ceremonials purified or given up. In the current East African revival a new commitment to personal fellowship across racial and cultural lines has been stressed. Everywhere witness-bearing is part of the demand.

Finally, sooner or later, comes a *crisis.* Some issue arises on which the traditional society and the Christian conscience are sharply divided. People are forced to take sides. They discover whether they belong most deeply to the old way or the new. Persecution makes some grip the faith more firmly, others fall away. Then the crisis passes and this process is repeated, perhaps at a deeper level than before.

It would be going too far to assert that Christian growth must always follow this pattern, though many of us could doubtless give examples of the process from our own experience. And it may be useful to remember that quiet growth in Christian maturity, understanding, and commitment are as truly part of our obedience as steadfast endurance in a crisis. The latter will not take place without the former.

A Reconciling Fellowship

Yet the fact of crisis and the need for endurance must not be overlooked. The Christian way is often a hard and stony road, especially in Africa. It involves personal decision, "standing up to be counted," in the face of age-long acceptance of tradition. Often it means breaking with custom and enduring criticism, ridicule, and loneliness. This is equally true whether it applies to an European Christian in South Africa who questions apartheid, or to an individual African taking his Christian stand against the pagan customs of his family, neighbors, or village. But suffering for the gospel, borne in patience and goodwill is a powerful witness to the truth of Christianity. Sometimes it strikes home with a tremendous impact, vindicating the sufferer in the strongest possible way; though this can never be foreseen in advance. The crosses confronting the Christian are real tests of faith and courage. Only by enduring them courageously, can he learn that the end of the way is life, not death.

In many places today the hardest cross the African has to bear is the attitude of the Europeans toward him. In this respect white Christians all too easily conform to the patterns of the society around them instead of standing with their African brethren.

A few years ago one of the colonial governments in Africa appointed an official to promote better public relations with the African population. The official, seeking the help of a group of African young men, proposed an interracial fellowship having as its symbol a pair of clasped hands, one black and the other white. The men asked to have the device explained. Then they said: "We cannot serve under a lying symbol. How many of your people would clasp our hands in sincere friendship? Until they do, this symbol would be a pretence. Our people would laugh at us if we were deceived by it. Let us be honest with each other, and make no claims that are not supported by the facts."

In multi-racial towns and cities African Christians are exposed to the scorn of the growing numbers of those who have lost all confidence in the European. White Christians, on the other hand, are under growing pressure to give up any attempt at genuine partnership across racial lines. To hard-headed realists on both sides, the Christian belief in reconciliation seems folly.

"The missionary came first," says the African. "Then followed the trader. Last came soldiers with guns to kill, conquer, divide, and rule. Missionaries were the means by which white people lulled Africans to sleep while they took away their land and their freedom. African ministers are traitors. They are paid for selling their brethren. What has Christianity done to improve our lot? What is it doing to fight the color bar?"

Harsh and unfair as this judgment may seem in the face of more than a century of devoted Christian service to Africa, it is all too fully borne out by the attitudes of many people today. There is, indeed, only one real answer. "We preach not ourselves," but Christ. In his sight we are all *sinners,* guilty of pride, exclusiveness, and selfishness. Only as fellow-sinners, daily experiencing the forgiving love of God, can we claim fellowship with those who have suffered at our hands. Here is the great fact of reconciliation in Jesus Christ that is the foundation stone of the Church. Only as Christians keep fellowship with one another, knowing that the man made barriers that try to divide them have been broken down in Jesus Christ "who has made of both, one new man in Himself," only so can the gospel of reconcilation prevail and the world be saved from futile strife. It is on this front, perhaps more than on any other, that the battle between Christianity and the paganism of the world that rejects Christ is most sharply joined today. As in New Testament times a dedicated minority is striving against tremendous odds. But shall not God prevail?

"Open on the God-ward Side"

Thus in at least five respects the young church in Africa reminds us of the New Testament church. It is the work of God, not a merely human achievement. It is a movement of people "belonging to the Way." As such a movement it is one body in Christ, and it seeks to make that unity more manifest. It is learning more and more what discipleship means. And finally by the witness of suffering it testifies to the reconciling love of Christ. These five characteristics might be summed up in one: the church, when it is most truly alive, is fully responsive to God's will and leading. In a moving preface to his translation of the Book of Acts, which he entitles *The Young Church in Action,* J. B. Phillips tells how he was impressed by this quality in the early church:

The reader is stirred because he is seeing Christianity, the real thing, in action for the first time in human history. The newborn church, as vulnerable as any human child, having neither money, influence nor power in the ordinary sense, is setting forth joyously and courageously to win the pagan world for God through Christ. Here we are seeing the church in its first youth, valiant and unspoiled—a body of ordinary men and women joined in an unconquerable fellowship never before seen on earth.

. . . This surely is the church as it was meant to be. It is vigorous and flexible, for these are the days before it ever became fat and short of breath through prosperity, or muscle-bound by over-organization. These men did not make "acts of faith," they believed; they did not "say their prayers," they really prayed. They did not hold conferences on psychosomatic medicine, they simply healed the sick. But if they were uncomplicated by modern standards, we have ruefully to admit that they were *open on the God-ward side* in a way that is almost unknown today.[1]

"Open on the God-ward side," that is the church as it was meant to be.

THE TERMS OF THE MISSION TODAY

Like other aspects of discipleship, the Christian world mission requires step-by-step obedience to the unfolding will of God. The way in which we are called to walk unfolds before us as we go. We cannot see very far ahead, but it is not necessary that we should. As James Russell Lowell sang a century ago:

> New occasions teach new duties;
>   Time makes ancient good uncouth.
> They must upward still and onward
>   Who would keep abreast of truth.

What are the marks of the Christian mission today?

[1] Phillips, J. B. *The Young Church in Action*. N.Y.: The Macmillan Co., 1955, p. vii. Used by permission.

A World-Wide Fellowship of Churches

On March 10, 1957, a great service of thanksgiving took place at Douala in the French Cameroun. It was Independence Day for the churches related to the Paris Evangelical Mission. Delegates from France read the documents by which the mission board and the church bodies in France handed over full authority to the churches in Cameroun. Representations of the Cameroun churches replied. The mission as a separately organized body passed out of existence; thenceforth the missionaries become "messengers" from the churches of Europe in the service of the Cameroun churches. The writer was present and spoke briefly in the name of the International Missionary Council. What was the appropriate message? Felicitations that the day of the mission had given place to the day of the church? No, not that. It was rather a message of rejoicing that the Cameroun churches would thenceforth be full partners in the task of Christian witness in a mission "beginning at Douala and unto the ends of the earth."

In one form or another events like this are taking place month by month all over Africa. The old pattern of Western based churches sending out missionaries as isolated witness-bearers among pagan peoples is no longer valid. Today the church is *there*. It is no longer accurate even to think of these younger churches as bridgeheads, won from the surrounding paganism, that will serve as bases for further advance for forces still to come from the West. They are much more than that now.

They are rapidly becoming full partners in our common undertaking.

Churches in Africa and Asia are sending forth their own missionaries. Missionaries from southern Ghana are working in the north, and missionaries from eastern Tanganyika in the west. A missionary from the Coptic Church in Egypt is serving in Sudan; and one from India in Kenya. Churches in Mozambique are sending pastors to the gold mines in Orange Free State. This is only a beginning, but it affirms the principle that all churches are partners in the world mission.

Since there are still great differences in size and wealth, a large part of the material resources and an important contribution of personnel must still come from the older and larger churches. But these may be more than matched in value by the vision and courage of the younger churches, by their ability to present the gospel in fresh and living terms, and by their readiness to endure hardship in the service of Christ.

Attitudes of paternalism and condescension, whether on the part of a missionary or a supporter of the mission, have become entirely out of place. There is a verse in Romans that suggests that the Apostle Paul learned, perhaps with some difficulty, to avoid a spirit of domination. "I long to see you," he wrote, "that I may impart to you some spiritual gift to strengthen you." And then he adds in a more brotherly tone, "that is, that we may be mutually encouraged by each other's faith, both yours and mine." *Mutual* encouragement must guide inter-church relationships from this time forward.

Leadership in the African Church

If the churches of Africa are to take their proper part
in serving and evangelising their own countries and as
partners in a world fellowship of churches, they must be
provided with a very much stronger corps of leaders
than they now have. In the whole continent of Africa
there is not yet a single graduate school of theology.
There are few good seminaries. Almost without exception such schools as there are suffer from depleted staffs,
small student bodies, poor libraries, and curricula
carried over from Europe or North America with little
creative adaptation to African needs. A few Africans have
studied for the ministry overseas. A very few others
have taken courses in the new university colleges in
Africa. Many have become able, effective Christian
leaders more by their own aptitudes, by experience, and
by the enabling grace of God than by any advantage of
formal training.

The church suffers because its able leaders are so few.
There might be considerably more, however, if many
able young men were not discouraged from the ministry
by lack of training facilities, low standards, and seeming
lack of opportunity.

All these factors and many more have been brought
out in a series of surveys of the training of the ministry in
Africa and Madagascar. These surveys that are so important to the future of the church were sponsored by the
International Missionary Council and conducted between
1950 and 1958.

The missions have been too preoccupied with other tasks, especially with basic general education, to give ministerial training the attention it should have had. Until recently it has seemed simpler and quicker to provide missionaries for the posts of higher leadership than to train a corps of African leaders able to assume such posts. Now it is becoming clear that missionaries are no substitute for African leaders standing within the life of their own churches.

Time and effort will be needed to make good this deficiency. One of the survey commissions recommended that not less than one-fourth of the total resources of the missions in staff and funds should be applied to leadership training at all levels. Nothing approaching this is being done yet. An important new development is the gift of two million dollars by John D. Rockefeller, Jr., to the International Missionary Council, which is being matched with an equal sum by a group of American mission boards. Of the total fund three-fourths is to be used to strengthen a score or so of the major theological schools in Africa, Asia, and Latin America. The rest will be used to strengthen the library resources of the seminaries through the selection, translation, and adaptation of needed works and the stimulation of new creative writing as well.

A special commission has been set up to administer this fund. It is hoped that this initiative will lead churches and missions to strengthen the many schools of lower grade which also have an essential share in training Christian leaders.

New Roles for the Missionary

These are not easy days in which to be a missionary. In many parts of Africa heightened tensions make mediation between opposing groups almost impossible. The ministry of reconciliation was never more difficult. Yet in just such a situation a board secretary made the following comment:

The calmness and determination of our missionaries amazes me. Working among black men, they have to undergo suspicion because they are white. And working with white men, they are scorned because they work with black. Ever more restricted in their activity, they constantly find wider avenues of service and contact. Here among them is no despair, no frustration, no regret at having undertaken one of the world's most difficult jobs, but only a conviction that it is a job to be done and a tremendous joy that they have been chosen to have a part in it.[1]

Furthermore as the church comes to maturity the missionary must resign posts of authority and leadership to Africans. As John Winslow wrote long ago in India, what is needed today is "not leaders, but saints and servants." It has been all too easy, through the years, for the missionary to "withdraw upwards" as Africans were called to fill the lower and more numerous posts of service. This concentration of missionary control in the key positions too often stands in the way of a real transfer of authority to the African church. At the same time this "withdrawal upwards" has resulted in too much ab-

[1] Reuling, John A. Quoted from a letter by permission.

sorption of missionary effort in administrative tasks while intimate contact with the people has been lost. John Taylor suggests "withdrawal sideways" as the right answer.

> Possibly the right place for the mission in these latter days is to be scattered abroad through the whole fabric of the church—some in secondary schools, a few in primary schools; some in the theological college, more in the parishes—simply in order to be fellow-members of the whole church, enriching it by bringing whatever gifts they have to the places where these hidden choices are being made. That is what very many African Christians . . . have said they would like to see. It is a pattern that might have been seen before, had the missionaries withdrawn sideways instead of upwards.[1]

If these changes make the missionary once again a yoke-fellow and even a servant in his relationships with African colleagues and the church, rather than a leader and master, it may involve suffering, but it places him again in the true succession of the apostles.

New Frontiers of Witness and Discipleship

Finally, the fellowship of younger and older churches serving in a common mission is sure to lead us all to areas of life still unclaimed for Christ. Geographical frontiers are vanishing. There are no longer great areas of the earth's surface without messengers of Christ. Untouched tribes are becoming hard to find. The call to "regions beyond" has lost its ring. Is this the end of the mission? Not at all. For in every land there are still vast

[1] Taylor, *op. cit.*, p. 29.

numbers of people who are still untouched by any *effective* Christian witness. The combined strength of all Christians everywhere is not too great for the work to be done. In fact the world's birth rate is still outstripping the church. The expansion of the church has not kept pace with the explosion of population now taking place. The task of witness-bearing remains urgent.

But even more urgent is the linking of the *extensive* outreach of the gospel with the *intensive* application of the mind of Christ to the whole of life. "Into all the world" also means "into every aspect of life." "The mission of the church" includes not only the missionary outreach in the traditional sense but all the other aspects of the church's response to God's call—concern with world peace and international relations, with race and ethnic tensions, with social justice and welfare, with delinquency, with marriage and the family, with health of mind, body, and spirit. All these are inseparable from the missionary witness. As John Taylor says:

> The true service of Christ's church, and the real understanding of persons, means seeing people, not in spiritual isolation, but in their total involvement in all the relationships and interactions of their environment. True love must take society seriously.[1]

Some of the ways in which African Christians need our help in this complex total task have been suggested in the chapters of this book. Other parts of the task rest primarily on Christians of America and the West, yet the insight

[1] *Ibid.*

of African Christians may help us face them; and the way we face them will surely affect Africa. Here are some of our challenges:

Scientists have been breaking through frontiers of knowledge from the fine structure of the atom on the one hand to space travel on the other. *What have the new science and Christian faith to say to each other?*

Power that threatens life itself has been placed in human hands, making international politics an awesome juggling with destiny. *What does Christian responsibility mean at this moment in history?*

A secular view of man, with no perspective beyond the world of time and sense perception, has dominated the social sciences for more than a generation. *Is Christian faith unconcerned with the moral climate that results from this?*

Criminal violence is vividly portrayed daily before the eyes of children on thousands of television screens. *Is this unrelated to the alarming rise of juvenile delinquency? Are Christian people content to have it so?*

Determined minorities of militant segregationists stand in the way of fair play and opportunity for Negroes, and the well intentioned majority do nothing about it. *Has Christian conscience lost its voice?*

These are some of the new frontiers that today's Western Christian pioneers must overcome. Only so can the gospel be carried "into all the world." Perhaps they seem far removed from Africa, which is the subject of this book, simply because they are *our* frontiers. But Africa is watching us. Many Africans would like to believe what we have told them about God, and Jesus Christ, and the way of love and truth. But a faith that seems valid only sometimes and in some places is not enough. Africans are looking to us for the validation of the Christian faith in our lives and our circumstances. In just this way we look to them and see that many of them *do* believe and the testimony of their lives confirms the power of the gospel.

There is one Lord and one faith. The mission too is one mission, and in the end we see that it is God's mission, not ours. Before we came on the scene He was there; after we are gone He will still be at work. For the little span of our lives we are privileged to share in His unfolding purpose.

In a memorable address at Ibadan, Bishop Obadiah Kariuki, of Kenya, showed that our fulfillment comes in knowing that Christ is Lord. Speaking on Christian family life, he pointed out that when the risen Jesus entered the home of the disciples at Emmaus it was He who took the bread and blessed it. It is the host, not the guest, who does this. So Jesus who entered as a guest became the host, and then they knew him. In all reverence we may say that this has happened in the mission of the church: that which we offered as *our* service he has taken up and made his own.

A Selected Reading List

LEADERS of study groups may order the Friendship Press books listed below from denominational literature headquarters. From these same sources, they may also order *Adult Guide on Africa,* by Edwin F. Tewksbury, priced at 50 cents, which contains program plans for using *The Way in Africa* and other Friendship Press materials.

Books of other publishers are listed as additional resources. The views expressed in them are not necessarily those of the author or publishers of *The Way in Africa.*

FRIENDSHIP PRESS BOOKS

Booth, Newell Snow. *This is Africa South of the Sahara.* An overall introduction to Africa, presenting both its problems and potentialities. Paper only, 75 cents.

Clemens, Gene Phillips. *Drum Call of Hope.* A challenging description of the medical and spiritual miracles performed by the American Leprosy Missions in Africa. Photographs. Cloth $2.95, paper $1.50. *Publication, Fall 1959.*

Horner, Esther D. *Jungles Ahead!* Six true stories of African young people. Rev. ed. Cloth $2.95, paper $1.50.

Karefa-Smart, John and Rena. *The Halting Kingdom: Christianity and the African Revolution.* A stimulating, sometimes sharp consideration of the church's mission in Africa by a Christian Sierra Leone official and his American-born wife. Paper only, $1.00.

Mathews, Basil. *Livingstone, the Pathfinder.* A great Christian writer's ever-popular biography of Livingstone. Cloth $2.75, Paper $1.50.

Nida, Eugene, and William Smalley. *Introducing Animism.* Another of the "Living Religions" series, this informative book is of particular value for the Africa study year. Paper only, 90 cents.

Ross, Emory and Myrta. *Africa Disturbed.* The impact of Western Christian culture on Africa as seen and told by Africans. A fascinating and up-to-the-minute collection, illustrated with photographs and drawings. Cloth $3.50, paper $1.95.

Ross, Emory. *African Heritage.* "Human Rights in Africa" and "The Christian Community and Mother Earth" are representative chapters of this popularly written book. A 1952 publication. Paper only, $1.25.

BOOKS OF OTHER PUBLISHERS

General

The American Assembly. *The United States and Africa.* New York: Columbia University, 1958.

Bowles, Chester. *Africa's Challenge to America.* Berkeley, Calif.: University of California Press, 1956.

Campbell, John McLeod. *African History in the Making.* London: Edinburgh House, 1956.

Gunther, John. *Inside Africa.* New York: Harper & Bros., 1955.

Hailey, M. H. *An African Survey, Revised 1956.* New York: Oxford University Press, 1957.

Perham, M. F., and Jack Simmons (comps.). *African Discovery: An Anthology of Exploration.* London: Faber & Faber, Ltd., 1957.

Sampson, Anthony. *Drum: The Newspaper that Won the Heart of Africa.* Cambridge, Mass.: Houghton Mifflin Co., 1957.

Stamp, L. D. *Africa: A Study in Tropical Development.* New York: John Wiley & Sons, Inc., 1953.

Stillman, Calvin W. *Africa in the Modern World.* Chicago: University of Chicago Press, 1955.

Wallbank, T. Walter. *Contemporary Africa: Continent in Transition.* (Anvil Book No. 15.) Princeton, N. J.: Van Nostrand Co., Inc., 1956.

Anthropology and Sociology

International African Institute. *African Worlds: Studies in the Cosmological Ideas and Social Values of African Peoples.* London: Oxford University Press, 1954.

Paton, Alan. *The Land and the People of South Africa.* Philadelphia: J. B. Lippincott Co., 1955.

Price, Thomas. *African Marriage.* London: Student Christian Movement Press, 1954.

Smith, E. W. *African Beliefs and Christian Faith.* London: Lutterworth Press, 1944.

Smith, E. W. *African Ideas of God.* London: Edinburgh House, 1950.

Van der Post, Laurens. *The Dark Eye in Africa.* New York: William Morrow & Co., 1955.

Race Relations

Akpan, N. U. *Epitaph to Indirect Rule.* London: Cassell & Co., Ltd., 1956.

Davidson, Basil. *The African Awakening.* New York: The Macmillan Co., 1955.

Hodgkin, T. L. *Nationalism in Colonial Africa.* New York: New York University Press, 1957.

Huddleston, Trevor. *Naught for Your Comfort.* Garden City, N.Y.: Doubleday & Co., 1956.

Oldham, J. H. *New Hope in Africa.* New York: Longmans, Green & Co., Inc., 1955.

Paton, Alan. *Cry, the Beloved Country.* New York: Charles Scribner's Sons, 1948.

Steward, Alexander. *You Are Wrong Father Huddleston.* London: John Lane, The Bodley Head, Ltd., 1956.

Taylor, John V. *Christianity and Politics in Africa.* (Penguin African Series, v.9.) Middlesex, Eng.: Penguin Books, Ltd., 1957.

Christian Missions, Yesterday and Today

The Church in Changing Africa. Report of the All-Africa Church Conference, Ibadan, Nigeria, January 1958. New York: International Missionary Council, 1958.

Considine, John J. *Africa, Land of New Men.* (Roman Catholic Missions.) New York: Dodd, Mead, & Co., 1954.

Groves, C. P. *The Planting of Christianity in Africa.* (4 vols.) London: Lutterworth Press, 1948-1958.

Oliver, Roland. *How Christian Is Africa?* London: Church Missionary Society, Highway Press, 1956.

Sundkler, B. G. M. *Bantu Prophets in South Africa.* London: Lutterworth Press, 1948.

Taylor, John V. *The Growth of the Church in Buganda, An*

Attempt at Understanding. London: Student Christian Movement Press, 1958.

Westermann, Diedrich. *Africa and Christianity.* New York: Oxford University Press, 1937.

Biographies

Mueller, John J. *Great Missionaries to Africa.* Grand Rapids, Mich.: Zondervan Publishing Co., 1941.

Nkrumah, Kwame. *Ghana.* New York: Thomas Nelson & Co., 1957.

Seaver, George. *Albert Sweitzer, The Man and His Mind.* New York: Harper & Bros., 1947.

Seaver, George. *David Livingstone, His Life and Letters.* New York: Harper & Bros., 1957.

Pictorial

Paton, Alan, and Dan Weiner. *South Africa in Transition.* New York: Charles Scribner's Sons, 1956.

Reich, Hans. *Portrait of Southern Africa.* London: William Collins Sons & Co., Ltd., 1956.

Schmalenbach, Werner. *African Art.* New York: The Macmillan Co., 1954.

Taylor, John V. *The Passion in Africa.* London: Mowbray & Co., Ltd., 1957.

ABOUT THE FORMAT

The text of this book is set in Caledonia 10 point leaded three points. This linotype face, designed by the late W. A. Dwiggins, distinguished designer, typographer, and illustrator, belongs to the "modern" family of type faces and is somewhat similar to Scotch Modern, although more freely drawn than that letter.

Manufactured by Book Craftsmen Associates, Inc., New York
Jackets and paper covers by Affiliated Lithographers, New York
Map by Louise E. Jefferson
Typographic design by Margery W. Smith
Binding by Louise E. Jefferson